George Matteson lives in
of Maine with his wife, art
and around NY Harbor and the Northeastern US coast and
inland waterways from 1971 to 1999, including running his
own tugboat, the Spuyten Duyvil, for 13 years. For some of
those years, he not only worked, but also lived on the
water.

He is the author of *Tugboats of New York: An Illustrated
History*, New York University Press, 2005 and
Draggermen: Fishing on George's Bank, Scholastic/Four
Winds Press, 1979, and the co-author of *The Christmas
Tugboat*, a children's book, Clarion Books/Houghton
Mifflin, 2012. He is also an accomplished poet, with an
anthology, *That Miraculous Land & Other Poems,* East
River Press, 1982. He curated an exhibition, As Tugs Go
By: A History of the Towing Industry in New York Harbor,
at the John Noble Maritime Collection, Sailors' Snug
Harbor, in Staten Island, New York in March, 2008

First published in the United Kingdom and the United
States in 2019 by Dalzell Press.

Dalzell Press
54 Abbey Street
Bangor, N. Ireland
BT20 4JB

ISBN 978-0-9563864-7-2

Library of Congress Control Number:2019947512

Cover image: Collection of the Author

Front Cover Design by Holly Gewandter

The events in this book took place. As memory is
sometimes fallible, dialogue is approximate. Some names
have been changed, and certain events have been reordered
or compressed in order to serve the stories.

Tugboat Stories

George Matteson

Dalzell Press

New York   Bangor, N. Ireland

For Evan

"American Flight 01 out of Newark"

He seemed shrunk, and neither he nor his threads recovered from last night's attack of hot suds. His old, sun cut, blue eyes struggled to suss out the deal with the numbered seats and the overhead bins. I was here to run interference for him but somehow he had gotten way out ahead of me and was in danger of running off the chart. He listened with great concern to the safety talk, particularly the part about the seat cushion, which he gave an expert pinch to see if it could possibly perform as described, and shrugged otherwise. Hands so big and battered they seemed immoveable, but by the time the nice ladies had done the cross check he'd twisted up a paper napkin to a yarn and formed it into a minutely decorative knot, a sheep-shank used to adjust the length of line, but useless against time.

"Hope this thing runs at least as good as my old Gwen-Ed," he said with a confidential grin, the name of his beloved boat pronounced to rhyme with squid.

I remember, the mysterious coal black investor, in spotless white and wind-whipped robes impervious to soil or salt spray. He'd chartered the boat for the day with no stated purpose; politely declined every offer of food or drink; just stood at the bow, gesturing blithely toward each tangled shore in its turn saying again and again "Ova-thay-ah!" and Ed's prescription: "Seeing how he bothered to come all this way from the Dark Continent I guess he gets whatever he wants."

The finely tapered blade of shadow wing runs ever faster beside us. It jumps a fence, scythes a weed lot, leaps across a stagnant ditch, only to be left behind like a Labor Day pup at the edge of the Kills. Our jet begins to bank to the east and the Harbor rolls into view.

"Oh my God, there she is," he exclaims as the Statue flips him her backhand salute.

And there, the Hudson forcing its vascular passage northward; and the entrails of the east River, all twists and tributaries leading out to the Sound. The glinting pinnacles of Manhattan. The Upper Bay and its spacious anchorage.

"And look at the Kills!" he cries as we sweep over Bayonne. A big container ship, bound for sea, ekes around Bergen Point with the assistance of two tugs, one on either side, set bow and stern, spewing white torrents of quickwater and barnfires of black exhaust as they midwife their charge to the salt.

Then the mythical places; the tugboat graveyards of Shooters Island and Rossville, the long-gone destinations

Port Ivory and the Mahogany Dock. Ranks and rows of wooden hulks abandoned to the mudflats; whose storied names were forgotten faster than their fabric.

"That's Ray Phelps' old DOTTIE E. down there. I beached her out back there, oh, maybe '65. We thought all the way she was going to sink out from under us any minute, then we got her there and she wouldn't. Took the whole rest of the night to get her down."

A great white heron lifts off from her rail and flies on slow wings toward the Isle of Dogs. The big company tugs thread their oil and chemical barges through the tight bends, past the refineries and the old killing fields of industry, past the vast mountain of city trash atop which tiny trucks and graders scuffle.

Where even garbage is a form of commerce at all hours, season and weather. 2 a.m. and 2 below and a bitter wind. A barge breaks loose and comes against another. A man is tossed into the sea. "He'd a been OK, he'd a just jumped down in the garbage...."

Then higher, banking leftward, faster, out over South Amboy, the big lonesome expanse of Raritan Bay, the Narrows and the channels, Chapel Hill, The Swash,

Ambrose, and Sandy Hook. The tall bluff and twin towers of Navesink still signal out to sea; their limits rather than their lights extinguished.

Forgive me now for talking fast, but things go pretty quick once they start.

He turned to me. He cupped his hands as if to conserve some water or an exhausted bird.

"It looks like it all could fit just here," he says. "I didn't know."

A Golden Fleece

Just a couple of days into the job Conrad Staus turned to me and with a perfectly straight face asked, "Hey kid, you ever fuck a sheep?"

"No," said I.

"Well, where I grew up, everybody did, all of the kids, that is, and most of the adults. Little cows, sheep, whatever you could find around the barn. They say the Amish even screwed their pigs but you'd have to ask them about that; the pigs, that is. This was before the sixties mind you; before the girls all got taught in school how to screw. Pennsylvania farm country where I grew up? No place like it!"

"Land of opportunity?" I said uncertainly.

He stared at me for a moment. "I get what you're saying," he said, "but I'm not sure I agree with you, but I guess that's why we're here in the big city, isn't it?"

In those days I lived simply; on a small decrepit wooden tugboat which I slowly improved even as I sought odd jobs around the harbor. I had built an accommodation into it for myself; a skinny bunk, a narrow desk, a coal stove for cooking and for warmth. I moored the boat at Pier 15, East River; the foot of Maiden Lane. At night I slept as the tides rose, then fell, then rose again. The constant traffic of tugs and barges set the water lapping at the pier and set my small home to endless rocking. Across, among the piers of Brooklyn Heights deepwater ships came and went at all hours, their horns playing back and forth between that high banked shore and the towers of Wall Street. The Fish Market slouched and bickered all night in the streets behind me; while across the river hard by the Brooklyn Bridge, the Jehovah's Witness' sign exhorted all the city and its waters, "Do You Pray? Read God's Word. Awake!" then gave the time and temperature.

In the first of the harbor dawn I would shake down the banked embers in the stove, pump water into the coffee pot and place it on the blacked and polished stove top where the heat would soon rise. I would step out on deck to piss over the side, to look up at the weather. In those days a few still lived on the waterfront. They denned in the marginally weathertight cabins of abandoned scows. They vacationed perpetually aboard ancient pleasure boats which never shook their moorings. On the mudflats they fashioned shanties at the end of spindly walkways. They clung to the proprietorship of tiny boatyards; tinkered endlessly with massive hulks they dreamed back to redemption. Every creek and backwater had its own little community of determined squatters. Some eking a living as watchmen, some pilfering copper, some trapping eels. These were of the tribe through whose hands nothing new ever passed.

For a time, when any of them needed something moved – whether it be a houseboat facing eviction, a leaky scow, a fender log, or a landing stage – I would be called. Each job was different, many were unusual even by the standards of that community; and some were downright weird. Most, at bottom, were founded on futile optimism. I would tow a worthless hulk to an expensive shipyard where it would be hauled out and deemed to be beyond redemption. An antique ferry haunted within by owls might be imagined as a sumptuous casino only to be at last condemned and towed to the knacker's. I undertook more broken dreams than Charon. The impulse was pervasive throughout the backwaters of the harbor. Everywhere lurked hard-bitten dreamers, all at work on something big. It would be safe to say that not a one of these dreams ever came to pass, but each sustained its dreamer for a time, and each in its doomed trajectory cast a feeble sparkle of commerce, some of which it was my fortune to pocket. I would charge them as little as possible to shuttle them back and forth across the Styx. I was strict as to the terms of payment, hoping to lay a good varnish of credibility over my scumble of a business. Though I dealt almost exclusively with fantasy, I liked to believe in those days that my little boat, my little business, my little life was not, like everything else around me, so... small.

So, in an effort to reassure myself, and with the help of what I imagined to be blind circumstance, I agreed to work for Conrad Staus, who's business card read "Vice-President & Field Engineer – Golden Fleece Construction" and who introduced himself as, "Staus, that's *S-T-A-U-S, one s no r."* He just appeared one afternoon on the dock wearing a white safari jacket, khaki pants, well-polished brown work boots and, atop it all, a stylish brown fedora. He was a big guy with a hard angular face and a thin moustache: Hemingway and in a hurry.

"I got six guys working out on Ellis Island and I need somebody to take 'em out in the morning and bring 'em back in the afternoon. There might be some more trips back and forth during the day, depending. You pick up at the Battery, 7:30 sharp, come get 'em at the island at 3:30. I'm paying $150 a trip, you keep track of the number of trips every week. Write out the number of trips at the end of every week. Just the number; don't put any dollar figure to it, and I pay you cash Friday afternoon. You want it?"

"Yes."

"You say yes, that means you're gonna do it."

"Yes."

"Good! Battery. Tomorrow morning. 7:30." And he was gone.

Damn, I thought. I just got myself a real job!

***

Next morning at 7:00 I had the boat standing by off the Battery well before the appointed time. The harbor was already busy at that hour. Right next to the Coast Guard pier where I was supposed to meet my passengers were the Whitehall slips, in and out of which the Staten Island and Governors Island ferries hustled the morning rush. Out toward the Statue, there was the normal round-the-clock tug traffic of oil, gravel, sand and trash; but also, coming out from behind Staten Island and from all along the Jersey side were the day-boat tugs setting out with a variety of floating cranes, construction equipment, railroad barges; while behind them an elephant parade of deepwater ships marched in through the Narrows, passing under the

13

Verrazano, meeting their docking tugs just off of Quarantine and proceeding into the Kills. A dwindling few – mostly those with cargoes of raw sugar, green coffee, or bananas - broke from this procession and diverted to the Bay Ridge shore, to Red Hook or toward the East River. In front of me, right around the massive granite curve of the Battery Park seawall, the shore side was also setting up for the day. Long poled fishermen lined up along the seawall fence, each attending several lines, patiently awaiting the favor of a bluefish or striped bass; but ready to settle for a hogchoker or a tom-cod. Joggers roved the paths, here and there a lonely Chinese danced Tai Chi; and all along stood quiet souls leaning on the railings, gazing at the water.

Right at 7:30 my passengers pulled up in a beat blue van. They tumbled out, dragging tools and baggage behind them, and filed down to the dock. I nosed the tug in, stepped down from the pilothouse to cast a docking line over one of the mooring cleats on the dock, made it fast to the stem post at the very bow of the tug, then climbed back into the pilothouse to run the engine at dead slow speed against this bow line to hold the boat tight against the dock while the men loaded themselves and their gear aboard. As promised, there were six of them, plus Staus himself, dressed exactly as the day before; safari jacket, khakis, and

14

fedora. He jumped aboard and climbed straight up into the pilothouse to join me. It was a warm morning and I had all of the windows open. He leaned out the one in the center and started urging the crew to speed up the process of getting on board. They gingerly climbed down from the dock, onto the tug's rail and then down onto the deck. They hesitated at each new stage like livestock negotiating unfamiliar chutes.

Conrad turned to me. "You speak Spanish," he asked?

"No'" said I.

"Neither do I and it doesn't matter. Most of these guys don't either. Matter of fact, I don't know what they speak. Seems like they all speak different. They maybe even change back and forth from one thing to another for all I can tell. Foreman's Mexican so he speaks Spanish, but he can't speak to any of the other guys, but it doesn't matter what you tell him even if you could. Name's Jose or Pedro or something. When I'm not here you deal with him."

. The crew itself didn't really resemble a work crew. Most construction gangs tend to have a sort of uniformity of dress, manner, and, depending on the management of the company they worked for, of national character and race.

Greeks tended to hire Greeks; Polish, Polish; Irish, Irish; and, whatever the nationality, they all usually wore clothing that suited the labor to which they were bound. Coarse pants; coveralls, perhaps; hats, hardhats, perhaps; and always, some sort of durable shoes – most in favor at this time, lace-up Timberlands. In addition to this basic outfit you would expect to find various accessories more or less specific to the particular trade. Iron workers wore belts from which dangled spud wrenches, Wescotts, and strikers. Carpenters carried hammers, tapes, and levels. Even general laborers might have gloves, leather or at least leather-palmed, particle masks, and ear protectors. There was the appearance in any given work crew that they were *equipped*; ready to do what needed to be done.

But the guys who climbed down onto the deck of my boat that morning were notably un-equipped. One was clad in a heavy ski parka though it was a warm early summer morning. Another was dressed in a tee shirt. One sported a button down collar that could have come from Brooks Brothers while the man next to him was clothed in what were almost rags, albeit rags of vibrant color. Their pants were just as varied with not a single blue jean or Carhartt among them though there was one man, he of the button down collar, who had somewhere acquired the baggy checked pants of a chef. Most were bareheaded; two had white cotton gardener's gloves. One wore black leather street shoes, four wore sneakers and one had flip-flops. And as if the miscellany of dress were not noticeable enough, their ethnic and racial mixture was another marvel. There was an Asian, possibly Vietnamese; a South Asian either Indian or Pakistani; an African American, a thin fellow with buzz cut sandy hair and a tired look who I guessed to be a Slav, a Pole, or maybe a Russian. There was an Arabic looking fellow – the one with the natty shirt and checkered trousers and, coincidentally, the flip-flops. And finally, there was the foreman, Jose/Pedro, a Mexican.

Only later have I come to understand the amount of effort that this gathering of souls must have required; and I wonder whether it was the result of some kind of complex hiring formula that derived from the requirements of bidding on this particular contract or was it just another of Conrad's amusements? Whatever the cause, the result was a foredeck packed with men crimped from all around the globe.

"All you motherfuckers, ready to go?" Conrad bellowed out the window. Most only flinched, while the Slav gave a melancholic thumbs-up; and we set out on the short voyage to Ellis Island. They sat along the rail of the

17

tug looking inward, eating out of their paper sacks, silent. And when the tug eased into the arrival slip at the island and nosed into the bulkhead there, they stood and filed straight in through the door of the vast reception hall where they would spend the rest of the day pecking away.

In those days Ellis Island was entirely abandoned and overgrown. It would be years before its redemption as the shrine to immigration. To explore there at that time was akin to discovering a Mayan temple deep in the Yucatan. Once an establishment of grand buildings in orderly rows set off by judicious plantings of ornamentals, hedge, and avenues of sycamore, the terrain in abandonment had become a riot of vines, bittersweet, Virginia creeper, poison ivy; and every species of rank exotic, honey locust, tree of heaven. And permeating everywhere there lay the sickly stench of privet gone wild. All of the buildings were in total disrepair with not a window nor a door still hung; every plaster ceiling had fallen and been ground to powder on weather buckled parquet floors. Myth ascribed to each of these ruined halls a purpose: the place of dental extractions, tuberculosis ward, nursery, morgue; but there was no trace left to prove these distinctions. Every structure, every room and floor was a uniform rubble of dust and shattered glass; and every scrap of metal, whether copper, zinc, lead, steel, or brass had long since gone over the water to Bayonne. Whatever the trials of those who had passed through the place and all of its specialized confinements and hermetic vaults for broken dreams, there was no remaining evidence. All of the ghosts had gone and my wandering self and Staus's little band replaced them, tapping and scraping away in the cockloft of the reception hall. I explored the island those mornings with the cicadas sizzling in the still heat, lost tribes of pigeons exploding from the gaping upper floors to vanish into the impenetrable summery glare of heaven.

***

Before long, the task of getting the crew to and from the island became entirely routine. Day after day I would rise early and enjoy the dawn as it marched down the broad straightaway of the East River. The sun rose over Greenpoint, Brooklyn; the Domino Sugar plant, the Navy Yard. Daylight tumbled through the three great bridges before spilling out across the Upper Bay. I would make coffee on the stove then sit in the pilothouse to drink it, looking out. The freighters across the way would be just rolling back their hatches with a rumble and booming that rebounded up and down both shores. Then they would limber up their deck cranes to begin their day of cargo operations. Other ships might be just arriving from sea with one or two tugs attending. Each ship would deliver itself to a position right off its assigned pier, at which point it would surrender itself to the tugs, which would heave the ship around to a right angle with the shore then carefully insert it into its berth. The ship and tugs communicated by soprano and baritone volleys of whistle and horn Most of the arrivals occurred sometime near dawn to be ready for the incoming gangs of longshoremen that would unload them. Each ship would stay two or three days to discharge cargo, then load. When done, they would call for the tugs whatever the hour to be on their way.

At twenty minutes before 7:00, I would leave my coffee mug on the window sill of the pilothouse and climb down the steep ladder into the engine room to start the engine. Usually it was still warm as the flank of a horse from the work of the day before. I would then go on deck to cast off the dock lines starting at the stern; taking in each line in turn and, coiling it down on deck, finally releasing the bow and backing the boat away from the pier for the short run down to the Battery. Because of the simplicity of this daily assignment I needed no deckhand.

The crew was always on time, tumbling out of their van with their coffees and buttered rolls, their sacks of oddments and tools. Staus was there sometimes, sometimes not, and over time the makeup of the crew would change with one man dropping out to be replaced by another. I never knew exactly what the crew was supposed to be doing on the island. It seemed that they were involved with repairing leaks in the roof of the main building, but none of the tools or equipment that they brought on board each morning seemed fit for anything more than the most rudimentary tradecraft. A couple dozen common brick, a can of tar, or roll of felt was all I ever freighted for them. The men had little more than claw hammers and trowels; and I never saw a power tool among them for there was certainly no electricity available out there. It was obvious that whatever these guys had been hired to do was insignificant in comparison to the vast shattered hulk of a building that they entered every morning at 0800 sharp and filed out of each afternoon at 1500. But to their credit they emerged at the end of each day looking a little more tired and a little dirtier than they had gone in. I grew fond of them as the days went by, seeing them as a ragged little band with scant resources struggling endlessly within that crumbling edifice – an edifice built in the grandiose style of the Renaissance Revival no less. I believe that they were unable to state the purpose of their labor. They worked simply because Conrad Staus allowed them to; his little flock of sheep.

***

I had been on the job for two weeks and was feeling good. It was a Saturday morning and I was up at the usual time, though there was no work that day. I walked up to get breakfast at the tiny Greek diner one block up from the Water on John Street. It was called The John Street Food Shop and was staffed only by the short order cook - a beat and burnt up old guy named Spiro who worked maniacally over his grille with his back to the counter. Whenever a customer entered the narrow hazy place he would glance quickly over his shoulder; most who entered at breakfast were either fish market or janitorial from the surrounding buildings. A very few of these would be treated to a brief greeting while all others Spiro would either ignore or else quietly mutter what sounded like a curse. The muttering would continue until a new customer came through the door, but all the time Spiro would be preparing the most recent customers customary breakfast. Fast as lightning he would squash the bacon under his meat press - a common brick. He would break eggs for scrambling, one in each hand, then whip them furiously in a bowl worn paper thin. Bread would fly from toaster to plate, receiving a fan of soft butter as it passed. All of the elements of the meal would assemble themselves on the plate, each seeming to arrive like magic from a different direction and then Spiro with a grim and dangerous look on his face would half turn from the grille and with a brilliant flick of the wrist skim the plate down the counter to his hungry client.

Spiro served his regulars without the exchange of a single word. The tedious process of menu study and ordering had become extinct in the evolution of Spiro's trade. I never heard him ask a customer what he wanted. Any newcomer had to call out his order to Spiro's back and to receive first the muttered curse and, later, the food. If the customer were shy or didn't know the customs of the place, he might wait an eternity until Spiro, boiling with frustration, would flare around with blood red eyes, no more than a two-count, then revert to the grille. If the newcomer didn't take that opportunity to blurt out his order, he would have to wait another eternity until Spiro would once again turn to him, each time more impatient, more bloodshot and wrathful. To walk into the place shouting my order seemed alien to me but, like so much else in New York, I learned to do it.

A few years later Spiro and his little hole in the wall disappeared. It was taken over by a Korean gentleman and his wife who enlarged and beautified the place by taking over the lease of the copy shop next door. Soon it was transformed into a bright little 24 hour restaurant. The wife would greet the customers at the door and seat them while the husband would proudly man the cash register and stalk back and forth to the kitchen to keep the crew back there in line. He had a temper and one morning belittled and dismissed an Albanian dishwasher who returned at the peak of lunch hour with a pistol. Without a word he shot the owner six times in the chest, tossed the pistol on the floor and sat on the front step to await the arrival of the police. The place closed shortly after that and was once again subdivided, the larger part reconfigured into a One-Hour Photo Shop, while Spiro's old den became a Chinese take-out.

I had finished my breakfast at Spiro's that Saturday morning and was headed back down to the boat, just walking across South Street and under the massive elevated viaduct of the FDR Drive when a big baby blue Cadillac rolled up beside me. The passenger side window hissed open; I bent down to look in and there behind the wheel was a small leathery skinned man dressed in a wool shirt, buttoned to the neck, a string tie with a Navaho silver and turquoise clasp, double-knit trousers and a weathered and oil stained olive-green baseball cap. It was Fred Kosnac, a long-established waterman who operated out of Pier 5 just down toward Whitehall.

"I'm driving around and I'm looking for company," he said to me. "Get in."

I hesitated. "I'd love to," I said, "but I've got to…"

"I've had my eye on you. You're not doing nothin'," he interrupted. "Get in."

We headed uptown on South Street, veered left on Allen, and after a series of abrupt course changes through the Lower East Side emerged onto Delancey, then cruised across the Williamsburg Bridge into Brooklyn.

"I see you tied up there on Pier 15 all the time and I keep asking myself, 'Why's he not working?' And I'm thinking now there's a kid that's knows what he wants to do but just doesn't know how to do it. You need to get busy!"

"I just got a job out to Ellis Island."

"Yeah, I know, I know. I see you going back and forth, back and forth, but you need some real work; something with some hair on it for Christ sake."

"I thought I was doing pretty well."

"Well I'm guessing you're not. I bet he's paying you next to nothing. What, $300 a day, am I right? Cash, right? I bet he's got you down with his boss for twice that. And he's got you morning and afternoon so's you got no time to do anything else, and he's got you carrying all his lumber and his brick and other stuff for nothing. You ought to be getting three times what you're getting, but, look, you got to start someplace. But there's no sense starting unless you do actually, get someplace."

Fred knew what he was talking about. He had started off in the '20s with only a rowboat. Odd jobs, salvaging bits of scrap here and there and slowly, over time he had prospered. A full scale launch service, hauling crew and freight to ships at anchor out in the harbor. He had acquired a floating crane and undertook to deliver machinery and heavy goods. He had operated shuttle boats from Manhattan out to the 1964 World's Fair site in Flushing. In other words, he was a small businessman, always alert to a new venture.

His offices were located in a plain little cottage mounted on a barge that was moored at Pier 5, East River. It happened to be the very same vessel on which scenes of "On the Waterfront" had been filmed, and it was a likely coincidence, because Fred himself had for much of his career been in the thick of the epic tussle that had afflicted the harbor through most of the 20th century. Open warfare over labor and commercial turf had made the waterfront a perilous place. Mere survival required caution, while success by any measure required either real crime or real courage. It was a time of threats and beatings, punctuated now and then by outright brutalities – a boatman, for instance, discovered at dawn, chained beneath a pier, inexorably drowned by the previous night's high tide.

Fred had weathered these challenges and now was living an easier life. His son was ably running the business and "old man Fred", as he was now called, was free to scheme as he chose. The entire Port of New York was his turf, and today, our first stop was down on the Greenpoint, Brooklyn shore of Newtown Creek. We pulled into the asphalt lot of a distribution warehouse for a supermarket chain. Fred drove across the lot and parked in the shade of the loading dock. He got out of the car and I followed.

"I just want to find out what they're up to," Fred said under his breath as he stepped carefully along the warehouse wall until he reached the corner. Here he flattened his back against the wall and edged to the corner itself, craning his neck around to get a view of the creek. He had come out here to spy on the Boylan Brothers, whose yard was situated just across the creek. They occupied maybe 300 feet of bulkhead lining the shore of Newtown Creek on the Long Island City side. Moored at the bulkhead was a small canal tug with a grinning leprechaun painted on its stack. The doors into its pilothouse and engine room were hooked open, showing that the boat was active, as opposed to many of the old tugs that you saw in the backwaters of the harbor, closed up and all but abandoned. Just astern of the tug floated a good sized deck barge with a Manitowoc crane mounted on it. The crane looked to be in good shape and ready to go to work. Fred also owned a floating crane, a very old A-frame derrick built on top of a deteriorated wooden barge, but it was definitely outclassed by this one just brought into the harbor by his arch rivals.

"What are those bastards going to do with that crane barge, I keep asking myself," he muttered. "It's been there three weeks now just sitting. Brought it all the way up from Norfolk; big rush and now it just sits."

Fred ducked back into the shade of the warehouse wall. "We better get going before they detect me, but I just have to check up on them every now and then. You never know what they're up to except you can bet it's no good."

Though every business in the harbor was accustomed to a certain level of competition, there were some rivalries that exceeded all bounds. The long quiet war between Kosnac and the Boylans was one of these. Both were small operations that specialized in dealing with what are sometimes called "marine difficulties" – unusual situations that require a specialized, ingenious, or quiet solution. Services which might be called for could include responding in the middle of the night to pump out a sinking barge, breaking ice around a dock in winter, locating some obsolete engine part, disposing of a derelict hull or even providing location services for a movie production. The common characteristic of all of these services is that it is usually not possible to give the customer a price before the service is complete and so the customer must be confident that the final bill will be fair and honest. Fred's business had prospered over many years because he had established this reputation for honesty. He never took advantage. But equally important, he had learned to trust his instincts and to turn down any job which he sensed could not be accomplished according to his well-tuned standards.

"You don't need that kind of aggravation," he said to me. And more to the point, "That guy Staus just smells of trouble. You know Boylan was taking him back and forth before you? My guess is they fell out because they were all the time just trying to screw each other and they just wore each other out. Then Staus comes to see me and I can't do anything for him because it'll stir up trouble between me and Boylan, so I sent him up to see you."

"Just to see what I would do?"

"Not so much that as you're new in the harbor and don't have all this old baggage you got to tip toe around. I figured you might as well start someplace. You didn't make the best deal in the world, but at least you made some kinda deal. You're not in a position to say no and you at least had sense enough to say yes. There's always next time. That's how you learn."

We were driving back now into Manhattan. We crossed over to the West Side. Fred made a stop in the Gansevoort Market to buy wholesale meat, leaving me to watch the car as it sat with engine running at the curb. After a few minutes Fred came back out followed by a young man in a white butcher's smock carrying two boxes piled high with meats and groceries. They put the boxes in the trunk. Fred tipped the boy from a roll of bills he pulled out of his trouser pocket and got back into the car. He carried a sausage with him from the trunk and handed it to me.

"Have a salami," he said. "They sell it pretty good in there and I'm guessing you could use a little salami living on that boat of yours. Never goes bad and you can eat it any time."

"Thank you," I said, "What can I...?" but he cut me off.

"Hey, forget it. It's only a salami," he said, pulling away from the curb.

We drove downtown on West Street, under the rusting hulk of the elevated highway. Several peddler's booths had recently appeared there, first selling Christmas trees but slowly evolving into year-round ventures selling house plants, flower pots, straw baskets, huge stuffed toys. One vendor had, alongside a six-foot teddy bear, a seven-foot suit of plastic knight in shining armor; upright, propped against its unsheathed sword. Fred hit the brakes and swerved to a stop in front of the booth.

"I've had my eye on that for weeks. What do you think?" he asked, leaning over to gaze out the window on my side.

"The bear or the knight?" I asked.

"The knight of course. What would I do with a six foot teddy bear?"

We got out to admire it. The shopkeeper, Lebanese perhaps, was eager to make a deal and in minutes Fred had once again pulled out his roll of bills. He was ecstatic, and the Lebanese was beaming. We loaded the prize into the back seat, but it didn't articulate like a normal knight, so we ended up having to lay it on the back seats, then roll down a window so its pointy feet stuck out. We continued down the West Side, around the Battery, and up South Street to Pier 15 where Fred dropped me off.

"That was fun," Fred said. "We should do it more often but in the meantime, don't let that prick Staus give you none of his salami."

He began to pull away, but then stopped and backed up next to me again.

"I forgot what I come up here in the first place to talk to you about which is I see you're all alone there living on that boat of yours and I've got this girl down at my place who's been hanging around doing odd jobs. I think she may be one of those hippies. I don't pay her anything but just let her stay on the boats. She's maybe got mental problems, I don't know – moody kind of – but she's OK and she knows how to work. So I was thinking that maybe you could use her up by you, give her a place to sleep and she could help out. Used to call 'em centerboard deckhands back in the old days. Lot less trouble than the men and useful for a lot more things if you know what I mean. I don't know what your situation is and it's none of my business but if you got any use for her just let me know."

"I… I don't really have anything for her, but thanks for thinking of me," I replied.

"I just thought you might be interested. She's dependable and what-not. Just a suggestion."

"Thanks, let me think about it."

"Do that, and come down and visit anytime." And Fred drove back down South Street.

I was not tempted by Fred's offer at the time. Fact is, I had no use for a deckhand, there was only one bunk on the boat, and I already had a girl friend – sort of. She was an artist who lived in a corner of her studio over on Fulton Street. She was from South Carolina and spoke with a beautiful lilting Southern voice. She may herself have had mental problems – moody kind of – but when she was happy she was radiant and at least for a time, when she was happy, she would seek me out. Some mornings that summer, while I was busy transporting my little band of workers, she was back in the cabin warm and asleep in my bunk.

She lived in her studio which was located in one of those Lower Manhattan loft buildings in which space could be rented for any purpose so long as it was never clear what that purpose was. An office, a factory, a studio, a monastery, or a bordello (for a while there was one of these on the second floor with a neon sign in the window advertising "Hair Pieces for Men".) Landlords in that part of town were not too concerned who they rented to so long as the rent was paid and there was at least a thin veil of deniability should the bribe takers from the Department of Buildings come around.

It was not strictly legal to actually live in this building but the artists who rented studio space there were constantly redefining what it actually meant "to live". There was no law that said you couldn't heat up a can of soup or a pan of bath water on a hot plate normally used to cook up a pot of rabbit skin glue. There was no reason that you couldn't have a mattress on the floor; for who was to say it was not an artist's prop? No reason that a spider plant couldn't hang in a sunny window. My friend lived in such a place; with heat five days a week, a toilet and sink down the hall, and no hot water. Her space had once been a tiny factory of some sort and its concrete floor sloped slightly downward from all sides to a central drain; and it was here in the middle of the room that I often watched her bathe, young, tall, and glistening in the floodlit halo of her studio lights, attended by such hand maidens as she could afford: a mirror, her paints, a scrim of canvas.

Most of the people that I knew then, in that place, were living at the verge of self imagining. It was not the style to fashion more than one existence at a time. There seemed to be very little community, no groups of friends, just cautious matings among the scattered inhabitants of that district which teemed with business during the day, then after dark to the thundering of storefront gates clattering down became a ghost town with only glimmers of light from high floors and the occasional sounds of the ships on the river.

***

But things were not running smoothly in my dealings with Golden Fleece. As the weeks wore on the make-up of the crew kept changing. The first draft of workers who had come aboard on the first day had all been replaced by the end of the third week. Pedro/Jose disappeared early on to be replaced by a sullen Belarus. The others left singly or else in small groups so that it was difficult to keep track of which newcomer was the replacement of which member of the original draft. The last to go was Darryl, the black guy, who as it turned out had only recently been released from prison but, though he struggled mightily, could not seem to shake off the tentacles of the justice system. He had been probably the most talkative of the group. He had an open honest face and a direct gaze which distinguished him from the rest. Out of every week that we worked, Darryl was normally absent at least one full day, as he was summoned over and over again to attend court and parole appointments.

"I'm trying to put my life in order, like they told me to. I've got a job, I'm back with my wife and my child. I'm doing everything that I can do to make myself right," he would say to me with growing despair in his eyes. "And they keep calling me in."

Staus was surprisingly accommodating with the situation. "He's got some things he's got to deal with. I understand," he said.

The last day Darryl went out to the island he said he had yet another court date the next day. "That judge do sure know how to fuck with a nigger," he said; and then he was gone.

And as if the steady rotation of workers wasn't enough, it became obvious that less and less work was being done. Where in the beginning the guys had carried a few tools and every day loaded a smattering of materials onto the tug, as time passed the men came and went empty handed. Usually, when I arrived in the afternoon to carry them back from the island, I would find the entire group asleep in the shade of the big plane tree beside the building. They would rise from the grass and drag themselves aboard, looking dejected.

And even though there was steadily less work being done, Conrad began scheduling me to make additional runs to and from the island during the day, paying at the same rate as for the morning and afternoon runs. But the additional runs to and fro seemed to contribute nothing to the project. Sometimes Conrad would meet me at the Battery to hand me a blank piece of paper which I would run out to Ellis, hand it to the foreman and that would be it. Other times he would send a message with the crew in the morning that I was to be at the Battery dock in the middle

37

of the day to meet somebody, but if nobody showed up, just go home and bill it, fairly enough, as a round trip to the island. Soon they were paying me maybe $2,000 a week in cash every Friday afternoon at the Battery pier. I was rollin' in dough.

Then Conrad had another idea. "Instead of me having to tell you every time to make an extra trip out to the island, just bill me for one extra trip every day. When I need you for any more than that I'll let you know."

"You mean, bill you even if I'm not doing the trips?"

Conrad looked at me like I had a booger hanging from my nose; then shook his head and walked away. For that week and the next I put in only for the trips that I had actually done. Conrad was not happy.

"I thought we were going to change the way we did the billing," he said to me.

"I wasn't comfortable with it," I said.

"Wasn't comfortable?"

"I don't want to get into that," I said.

He stared at me. "And here I thought you were gonna be my guy," he said more or less to himself. "You know now I'm gonna have to find somebody else?"

"That's OK. I apologize if I caused you any trouble."

"You apologize?" He stared at me in disbelief then muttered "Stupid fuck!"

By the middle of the next week I was off the job and the Boylans had the work back. The next Saturday Fred was once again waiting for me in his Caddy under the FDR.

"Come down to the office; I want to talk with you about something," he said with a twinkle. "And I still want to introduce you to that centerboard deckhand of mine."

Some Birds

We were hanging on at the ship dock in Bridgeport. The big Manitowoc crane that they used for unloading containers filled with bananas had suffered a terrible calamity. The operator, while taking a strain on a loaded container, had allowed the boom to just kiss the rail of the ship. The crane was rigged with 120 feet of stick, so as to be able to reach out clear across the deck of a ship moored alongside the pier and, at full extension, pick a fully loaded container. Rigged like this the crane was maxed out and that tiny bump against the ship's rail – the slightest deflection of the boom lattice – was enough to fold the whole thing up. Simultaneously, the stick shattered at the heel and in the middle. The back ropes tore out of the cab, and the boom lay down over the deck of the ship like the arm of a snoring lover. The container plunged into the harbor on the outboard side of the ship. No one was hurt, thank God, but the crane was destroyed and, worse, the ship detained.

To get another crane up and running as quickly as possible, they hired a tug – me – and a barge in New York with orders to go up into the Harlem River where there's a crane leasing outfit located right on the river bank. Once there we shoved the bow of the barge up hard against the seawall and held it there with lines and the power of the tug. The crane guys set wooded mats on the deck of the barge and then, when the tide brought the deck of the barge up level with the top of the seawall, they drove the new crane aboard. When the weight of the crane came onto the barge the whole thing dipped and looked dangerous, but I'd never heard of a crane actually falling in. Though they may look ungainly when they try to walk around, cranes are actually very sure-footed.

Once it was on the barge, the crane guys secured it with cables and turnbuckles and then overnight we towed it out to Bridgeport. It was a clear calm night and the trip was entirely routine. We arrived just around sunrise and landed the barge down at the far end of the pier away from the ship. A watchman in a dirty green sedan with a yellow flashing light on top drove down the pier, stopped and looked at us for a while but didn't get out and soon went away again, which suggested to me that we were in the right place. The container filled with scared bananas was tied to the pier just in front of us, floating glumly on its cargo. The tide was falling so we were faced with a wait of almost eight hours before the next high tide would bring our barge up high enough on the pier to walk the crane off.

I shut down the engine and we slept for a couple of hours, then got up again, just about the time the longshoremen were arriving for work. I went up to the office to let the manager know we were there.

"You're not supposed to be here until this afternoon," he said, confusing me with the next high tide.

"I came out overnight. If we've got to wait we might as well wait here," I told him and then the deckhand and I took a walk up the street to the diner to get some breakfast. It was a nice late summer morning with a smoky haze and the spooky buzz of cicadas ever present. We walked through block after block of abandoned one and two family houses, doors beat in, windows beat out and stuffing-blown furniture all over the weed-filled yards. It looked like there'd been a long slow riot. Farther up, near the Jai-Alai parlor, there was a fruit stand with a big sign on the marquee which declared, "I'd rather go to jail for shooting you than you go to jail for shooting me." Not too many years before it had been almost suicidal to walk through these streets, but now everybody was gone. It had become a total wasteland and it seemed pretty safe; Hell of a town, Bridgeport!

On the way back after breakfast, we were walking back through the same devastation when there was a

43

rushing sound overhead, a burst of raucous cackling, and a flash of green. Five maybe eight birds rocketed by, screaming and chattering like little maniacs. I didn't get a good look at them but they had to be some kind of parrots.

By the time we got back to the dock a couple of guys from the crane company plus an operator and an oiler had arrived and were removing the lashings and getting the machine started up. The tide was just beginning to rise and wouldn't be high until two in the afternoon so everything that we were doing now was just in the way of killing time. My guess was that they planned to get the crane ready to go, then disappear until it was time to actually walk it off, maybe spend the middle of the day at the Jai-Alai parlor. I went down into the engine room to check out the engine, while the deck hand got busy cleaning up the pilothouse and the forecastle and all of us were looking forward to a slow morning, waiting on the tide. But just as I was coming back up out of the engine room there were those birds again. I heard them first, then caught a glimpse of them, shrieking down a row of aluminum sheds, banking hard over a rooftop, rolling hilariously, and gone. I guessed they might have come north on one of the banana boats, but that idea required that in just a few months, with the coming of winter, they must die.

Just as I expected, the crane guys disappeared. I had intended to talk to them about what time we should reassemble but apparently they had figured it out for themselves. All I had to do was sit around until they reappeared. I went up to the pilothouse to read and to try to get another hour or two of sleep because I would be up all the next night, towing the unloaded barge back to New York. The deck hand was already in his bunk down in the forecastle. Stretched out on the pilothouse settee I fell asleep easily and dreamed of the jungles of Brazil, of bananas, and of brightly colored birds. I awakened sometime later to the sound of the deckhand down below, rattling dishes around in the sink.

Up on the wharf there was a long black automobile. It had dark-tinted windows rolled up tight so I couldn't see if there was anyone inside but the motor was running to keep the air conditioning going. The tide had come back about half way and the crane guys were back, sitting on the stringpiece of the dock, their legs dangling over the edge, gazing down into the grey-green water. They were looking for the best spot along the length of the pier to walk the crane ashore; which section of the pier would best bear the weight – 250 tons more or less tricked out as it was with all the boom and counterweight it could carry. Looking at the surface of the wharf couldn't tell us much about what its condition was underneath where it really mattered, but we kicked around in the dust for a while trying to look conscientious because we guessed that the manager might be sitting in that big black car. After we settled on a likely looking spot we saw that, yes, the manager had gotten out of the car though the windows remained tight shut and the air conditioner continued to run. Everybody put their heads together and agreed on the spot to walk the crane off.

Later, when the barge was nosed in against the dock and all the mooring lines were set up and we were just waiting for the last few inches of tide, the operations manager, the crane guys, and I were standing in a group, and I asked whether there were any parrots hanging around the dock area? Off one of the banana boats maybe?

"We got nothing like that around here," the manager replied.

"I seen some kind'a birds just now, makin'a racket," the crane operator said.

"Those are Monk Parakeets from Argentina," the oiler replied. "They escaped from Kennedy airport maybe ten years back and now they're all over. There's a big colony of them over in the city park in Black Rock. It's a big ball of sticks up in a tree and there's at least a dozen of 'em living in it."

"There you go," the operator said while the manager stared out across the harbor.

Right at the top of the tide we got the crane safely ashore, and in just a few minutes I was headed back to New York with the tow. Meanwhile the crane operator had hooked onto the drowned container full of bananas, lifting it very slowly – barely faster than the falling tide – so that the weight of the seawater could drain out of it as it rose. The oiler stood off to the side and carefully watched. The black car with the windows rolled up was still parked on the apron with the manager inside.

Like Navigating a Sponge

We caught up with the ship just as it passed under the Bayonne Bridge. I throttled back and fell in behind it as the two attending tugs got into position to wrestle it around Bergen Point. One tug ranged up to the ship's bow on the port side while the other set its bow against the ship's starboard side back toward the stern. As the ship ventured into its turn the tugs angled in hard against the massive vessel and forced it around until its bow was aimed up the channel into Newark bay and the unloading cranes of Port Elizabeth. The ship had sailed from Hamburg with a full load of containers, each stuffed with everything imaginable except for the very last tier, right back at the stern where, in the space that would have been occupied by four standard boxes set two over two, there was an object cradled in an elaborate steel frame. It was shrouded in a sky blue tarpaulin sewn to a custom fit. It looked sort of like Grover Cleveland asleep in sky blue pajamas, contained in the cage of a giant bird.

"You said it was big, but I thought you were just talking normal big," said Trevor. "If that thing's as solid as it looks it's got to be 150 tons easy."

"180, I'm told," I said, "but all we've got to do is push it through water."

"Yeah, but it's going to be some pretty skinny water," said Trevor. "That canal fills in a little more every year and pretty soon you won't be able to paddle a canoe up there."

"I called them last week and they swear they've got nowhere less than nine feet of water and we're figuring this thing will be drawing not much more than eight so we should be OK."

***

We were only one element in a complex job. The generator had been ordered for a power plant just west of Syracuse in upstate New York after competitive bidding from firms in Europe, Japan, and the United States. It was built in a German factory by mostly Turkish workers, transported across the sea by a Korean ship manned by Danish officers and a Malay crew. After unloading in New York harbor and its placement in the barge, it was our part of the job to move it as far as it could go by water, that being the Erie Canal Terminal at the foot of Lake Onondaga: Syracuse, New York. There it would be shifted to a house mover's platform to make its final creep overland, to where exactly, it never occurred to me to ask. We had orders to bring the barge to meet the ship; to assist with the unloading of the thing; to get it safely to Syracuse; to help unload, and then to leave the barge secured at the terminal. After that we were free to deadhead back down to New York light tug. It was a rush job as it was already mid-November and the canal was about to close for the winter. The generator had been delayed in construction and they needed to get it to wherever it was going before winter set in. I had bid on my part of the job – the towing – about a year before. I'd been told that I'd got the job, but then had heard nothing more until just five days ago; at about the same time the ship had sailed from Hamburg. The job was on and my pick-up was first thing Tuesday morning with delivery expected at Syracuse first thing the following Monday – a generous amount of time so long as everything went according to plan.

It would be an 11, maybe 12 day trip up and back. The only thing unusual about it was that we would be leaving the barge up there once it was unloaded rather than towing it back to New York. I suppose that the Power Authority was planning to transport some other big piece of gear back out in the near future. I was hoping to get a chance to bid on that job when it came up, but first off, I had to do this one and in the five days between when I got the call saying the job was on and now, chasing the stern of the ship into Port Elizabeth, there had been a long list of things that had to get done. Food, water, diesel fuel, lube oil, and spare filters for both the main engine and the generator to be rounded up. Regular customers in the harbor to be called to make sure there was no upcoming work that might fall during the time I would be away and, if so, how could I cover it for them, either by doing it before or after, or in the worst case, by finding somebody else who would fill in without trying to steal the customer altogether.

But the biggest thing I had to sort out before I left was that I needed a licensed mate to go along. The Coast Guard had recently been getting serious about the rule that if a tug was going to operate more than 12 hours in a day there must be two people on board with licenses. In the normal course of harbor work I was rarely underway more than 12 hours in a day and even if I sometimes went over it was not such a big deal, as it was for truck drivers or railroad engineers. The Coast Guard didn't make a big deal of it so long as there were no accidents. I normally worked in the harbor with just myself and a deckhand on board. But to head off on a two-week job running around the clock would be a serious violation and if, God forbid, there were an accident, I'd be screwed; so I had to find somebody with a license to go along. Sometimes this is easy and, at other times, for reasons that are impossible to predict, it is difficult. I had a list of guys who I could call and this list was roughly graded from the best guys at the top to the worst at the bottom. The competence scale ranged from guys who had long years of experience on tugboats, to maritime academy kids who seemed to have found their licenses inside a box of Cocoa Puffs. These latter candidates could never be trusted to steer without close supervision, but because they had the necessary document they were still valuable if I got into a bind, even if you never dared let them touch the wheel and the only thing they did on the boat was eat, sleep, and talk about how they would rather be running an ocean liner.

This time I went through my whole list and came up empty handed. One after the next, each guy had some reason why he couldn't go, some of which sounded real and some of which sounded like they just weren't interested at the moment. Boatmen are an independent spirited crowd and will always seem to reserve for themselves the right to act on a whim whenever they can.

So after going through the whole list top to bottom, I did the only thing I could think of – I went through the list again, top to bottom, asking each if he really didn't maybe want to go after all and then, if the answer were still no, then did he maybe know anybody who might?

That's how I got Trevor's name. I was told that he had practically lived up on the canal for many years working for Eklof, Sears, and even for Matton way back. I'd be lucky to get him, I was told, and when I called him he jumped at the chance.

"I've been stuck down here in the harbor now longer than I can remember. I'd love to sail up there with you. Just tell me when you want me on board and I'll square it up down here."

And so, this morning, I met Trevor for the first time as he climbed down from the dock onto the rail of the tug in the light of dawn. He was dressed in a blue windbreaker with no pins, badges, or logos on it. He had on well-polished brown work shoes, brown corduroy pants and a tan ball cap, again without insignia or logo. He carried an overnight bag in one hand and a paper bag of take-out coffee and doughnuts in the other.

"Here," he said with a smile as he handed me the bag of coffees, "I figured these might help us get going."

"Yes, indeed," I said. The engine was running. Delbert Flynn, Del for short, my deckhand at the time, cast off the dock lines and coiled them down on deck and we headed out from Red Hook, Brooklyn to meet our ship in the Kill Van Kull.

***

"So what is this thing we're picking up?" Trevor asked as we steamed toward the Kills through the Back Channel.

"I'm told it's a turbine generator for a power plant they're rebuilding just outside of Syracuse," I said. "Too big for the trucks or the railroad."

"That's what I like to hear," said Trevor. "Anything takes work away from the roads and the rails is good. I keep waiting to hear they're going to close the canal and just let Conrail and the New York State Thruway fight over the real estate. Any time a job like this comes up I figure it postpones the inevitable for another year or two."

"I tell you, I'd sure be sorry if the canal closed down. I seem to get a couple of jobs a year up there. It's a big part of my business", said I.

"You're lucky. There's a lot of companies used to do nothing but work up in the canal and now there's nobody making a steady living up there and just a couple like you who make anything at all out of it. I tell you, I first started working up there and I'd still be up there if I could. You don't know how I've been looking forward to this!"

Trevor turned to Del, who stood at the back of the pilothouse, leaning against the chart desk. "What do you think there, Del? Captain here let you have any fun on these expeditions?"

"Ugh," Del replied in his half strangled voice. "Cap'n, here, doesn't know the meaning of fun."

"Uh-oh, that's not good," Trevor said with a laugh. "We're going to have to work on that."

"You can try," said Del. "I gave up."

***

We trailed along behind the ship and its two tugs until they started their turn into the channel up into Port Elizabeth, while I continued past to run into the neighboring slip of Port Newark where we were supposed to pick up the barge in which we would be transporting our cargo. I gave the steering over to Trevor while Del and I went out on deck to handle lines.

The barge was lying up at the head of the slip, and to get there we passed the whole array of business for which Port Newark is not all that famous. While Port Elizabeth, just half a mile away, is devoted almost exclusively to container ship traffic and appears to be very orderly and sort of futuristic with its spindly angular cranes projecting out into space and both the shore and the vast sleek ships all stacked with containers bright like poker chips in an epic wager, Port Newark is all about rust and grit. At the entrance to the channel, running in, there is a stretch of wharf on the right where car carriers lay with their stern ramps sloped ashore, disgorging autos one by one, like a termite queen laying eggs. Across the slip, on the other side is a vast scrap yard where the remains of the previous generation of automobiles were being clawed aboard ragged ships bound for the Orient to be smelted back into cars. Some of the ships themselves were bound to ship-breakers' yards in Bangladesh; sailing one last load of scrap to the East, and then the last empty voyage to the muddy shore of their own Resurrection.

Beyond that, a floating concrete plant on the left, a temple of dust lain idle, and on the right a massive dredge being overhauled, sporting here and there bright geysers of fire from the cutters and welders crouched at their hot work in the labyrinths of girder and pipe. A salvage tug waits for excitement. A fleet of idle sand scows ponders something big. And way up at the very end lays our tow, a small, boxy barge, which, being empty, sits up so high in the water that it seems a little bit topsy-turvy, out of trim. It is a LASH barge, an amphibious cargo box designed to be loaded with cargo and then carried in stacks on seagoing ships to be relaunched at the port of delivery and taken in to be unloaded, while the ship goes on its way. Because they were never intended to be anything more than a floating cargo container, to be towed only the short distance from the delivery ship to a nearby wharf, these barges have not the slightest streamlining and are famous for being inordinately slow and unwieldy. But apparently it was just the right size to carry our generator. The power company had purchased it outright for this job and intended to hang onto it in the event that there were more of these objects to be transported. It was freshly painted in blue and on each of its sides, in white, was the logo of the power company and the slogan "ENERGY FOR TOMORROW!" The logo and the slogan were drawn out in the largest lettering that could possibly fit on the sides of the barge.

"Fancy," I said as we approached.

"I didn't know a plain old Lash barge could look so pretty," said Trevor. "But it still ain't going to tow for shit."

Awaiting us, standing on the barge, was Nick Decker, the foreman of the yard.

"We prettied it up for you," he said as we nosed up to it. "The buyer came down the other day with this design and had us paint it on. Hope it's had time to set up. I think they're going to be a little disappointed when they put the weight into it. I tried to explain it to 'em but they didn't want to hear it."

"Least you told 'em so," I said.

"Tried to anyway. Boss picked this thing up, oh maybe five years ago, thinking he'd find some charter work for it, but it's been nothing but laying around all this time until these people come and snapped it up. Piece of shit, far as I'm concerned."

"Well, now it's our piece of shit so I guess you can let it go. What lines come with it?"

"Oh yeah, the new owner had us put four nice lengths of line on board. Brand new rope. You should be all set."

"OK," I said. "Del, if you and Nick could let her go, we'll be on our way. Trevor you want to take it out?"

"Sure, I guess so," said Trevor. "Just you tell me if I'm doing anything wrong, hear? I see we've got the one line up there on the corner. You thinking to yank it out on the one and flip it around before we get another line up?"

"Yeah, that'll work."

"Sounds good to me," he said and ducked into the pilothouse to man the controls while Del and I stayed on the foredeck to handle lines.

Trevor handled the maneuver nicely, particularly seeing that he had never operated the boat before and didn't yet have a feel for the weight and power of the tug and the speed at which it responded to throttle and clutch changes. He seemed able to judge just the right amount of power to use to get the barge to do what he wanted, and he kept a careful eye on Del and me as we handled the lines so that he didn't start to lay on power before we had the lines fully made up to the bitts. Clearly, Trevor was a boat handler.

We came back out the Port Newark Channel with the Lash barge alongside and made the turn back down to Port Elizabeth at just about the time our ship was getting the last of its dock lines ashore. Down Newark Bay, right by the turn at Bergen Point, we could see a big crane headed up toward us; most likely the machine that was going to be making the lift from the ship into our barge. We were scheduled to get the generator off the ship from the offshore side before they began unloading containers on the inshore side using the big port cranes. Neither the port nor the ship liked to wait around for anything, we were on a tight schedule, so I was glad that the crane assigned to the job was coming in a little after me. It was being brought by the THOMAS BROWN, a small tug that specialized in moving equipment around Ports Newark and Elizabeth. Its normal days work usually involved shifting dozens of scrap barges, sand scows, and floating cranes from one place to another in the port. Its captain and crew were easily the most skilled in the entire harbor. As they drew closer with the crane this morning, I could see that they were pushing it with just one line out from their bow to the middle point of the crane's hull. To move a heavy crane by this method, through the crowded waters of the Kill Van Kull, requires a confidence in your skills that no one else that I know of would assume.

"I love those guys," I said to Trevor.

"They make it all look easy," he replied.

We waited for the THOMAS BROWN to bring up the crane and to get it into position along the side of the ship. The plan was that the crane would be positioned so that its boom could swing directly over the load, pick it, then swing over the deck of the crane, lower the load to just a few feet of the deck and continue to swing in the same arc until it was positioned directly over our barge, then down until its entire weight was afloat: one slow, steady move.

Trevor eased our barge into the position indicated by the crane foreman, then we cast off from the barge and backed half a boat length away and tied up to the crane. A Jacobs ladder had been dropped down from the rail of the ship to the deck of the crane 30 feet below, the hard-hatted heads of two swarthy sailors peered down from the height as two of the men from the crane climbed up to set the bridles. The sailors helped them over the rail and out of sight and then a couple of minutes later they appeared on top of the load, silhouetted against the sky. The boom of the crane swung into position above them and one by one they shackled the four heavy wire bridles into the lifting eyes distributed around the circumference of the generator's cradle. Meanwhile, stevedores began to release the tie-downs that had secured the load during its voyage across the Atlantic. The crane took a light strain and the operator adjusted the position of the boom so that it was exactly over the load and then, when everyone had signaled that they were ready, the lead man of the two who had secured the bridles stood by the ship's rail, raised his right arm and with forefinger and thumb made a gesture that looked like one that you might make while examining the stickiness of honey, tapping thumb and fingertip together delicately, and then the engine of the crane throttled deliberately up to a steady roar and gradually increased the strain. The hull of the crane barge began to heel over under the increasing lever arm of the load and twice the lead man on the ship halted the hoist to top up the boom a little bit to bring the hook back into position directly over the load. Finally, with the hull of the crane heeling over maybe ten degrees, the load came off the deck. The lead man now switched from tapping thumb and forefinger together to holding his arm and hand vertical and waving his forefinger in a circular motion. The operator of the crane began a slow steady lift until the generator was above the level of the ship's rail and the lifting stopped. The air brakes of the crane winch set with a shrill yelp and the boom began to swing the load off the ship until it was clear of the rail, and once it was safely over the deck of the crane, to sequentially lower it and swing it further toward the middle until the load was about six feet off the deck and directly over the centerline of the crane and everything was straight and level. As soon as the load had gotten clear of the rail of the ship the lead man who had been directing the lift from his high vantage point had surrendered the job of signaling to the foreman on the deck of the crane. He now continued the swing of the load across the deck until it was right over our barge. Then he began to gently lower it until it barely made contact with the wooden sleepers that had been set across the deck of the barge's hold. Slowly, ever so slowly, the load settled down on the barge and slowly the barge settled deeper and deeper into the water. It's freshly painted blue sides sank into the silty green harbor tide.

"When's it going to stop?" asked Trevor as the nicely painted logo and optimistic script began to disappear.

Down and down it went. The foremen on the barge was now standing where he could look down into the barge, craning his neck out over the side, all the time signaling to the operator to keep on lowering slowly. The middles of the *E*'s sank, and by the time any slack appeared in the fall of the crane, the only thing left of the text was the very tops of the characters, the short dots of the very tops of the stems of the I's and the L's and the longer dashes formed from the remnants of the S's the T's and the O's. The theme of our voyage had been reduced to some new sort of telegrapher's code.

"Pretty near s-shunk it," said Del.

"You can say that again," I said just to see what would happen.

"Pretty near shunk it," said Del.

Trevor glanced at Del with a look of alarm.

The foreman from the crane climbed onto the barge with the surveyor from the insurance company. They stood looking down into the hold where the laborers were starting to lay out the cables and turnbuckles that would secure the load. I climbed off the tug to join them.

The surveyor was leafing through a clipboard of papers, The foreman had out a tape measure and was measuring the distance between the water level and the deck of the barge. There were only about 24 inches of freeboard, three feet of flat deck and then a 12 inch coaming around the opening of the hold to keep the whole thing from going to the bottom like a set of car keys.

"....it's the weight of the cradle, I'm thinking," the foreman was saying.

"I think you're right," said the surveyor. "I think that when they first sent the specs they were figuring to build lifting eyes into it but then decided to use a cradle instead. That would explain the difference."

"What you want to do?" asked the foreman. "Another barge?"

"That won't work. If it's on a deck barge it's too high to fit under the bridges up there. The whole thing is based on exactly this barge." The surveyor turned to me. "We're a bit deeper in the water that we figured. Supposed to be three feet of freeboard but turns out to be only maybe two. You think you can tow it that way?"

"I wouldn't take it out to sea, but it should be all right for the canal so long as we watch the weather," I said.

"You got a pump you can put on it if you need to?" the surveyor asked.

"Inch and a half gas pump," I answered.

"Plenty of gas?"

"Picked up five gallons just before we left," I said.

"So, you think you'll be OK?"

"Yeah, just remember though; if I have to hold up for weather someplace along the way, I had a good reason."

"I'll put a note in my report that you've got absolute discretion. Not that you don't anyway," said the surveyor. "Just, for God sake, don't lose it someplace. Do whatever you got to do."

***

It took another hour for them to finish up securing the load, and just before noon we were ready to start upriver. Trevor and I would steer in alternating six hour watches; the standard harbor routine of noon to 6 p.m., 6 p.m. to midnight, midnight to 6 a.m., and, finally, 6 a.m. to noon. I would take the afternoon watch, while Trevor and the deckhand would have the other. This would give me the midnight to 6 a.m. watch which is always the most difficult and thus the one that I felt obliged to steer. Del would stand his watch with Trevor who, being unfamiliar with the details of the boat, could use the assistance, and, who knows, might need somebody around to keep him awake. I'd never worked with the man so I couldn't be sure. Whatever the reasons, I generally preferred to stand my watches alone. If you had somebody sitting up with you there was always the risk that you would have to spend six hours talking, which is about the most exhausting thing I can think of; plus talking that much can give you a terrible sore throat.

I was wondering how Trevor would respond when I told him how I was going to break up the watches because there is some protocol involved. Normally, the captain takes the 6 – 12 watches and the mate stands between 12 and six, morning and afternoon on the theory that the midnight to 6 a.m. slot is the best time to sleep and so that time off should go to the senior man, the captain. I wondered that by taking what was traditionally the mate's watch whether I might be surrendering some authority to Trevor or sending a signal that I didn't trust him which, seeing how I'd never worked with him before, I didn't. But when I set it out to Trevor he seemed fine about it, and there was nothing in his response that I could read.

"Whatever way you want to do's fine with me," he said. "Actually, whenever I'd be going up the river I'd always do the same because half the time you get into the fog about half way through the watch and you end up tying up and going to sleep anyway." So, all afternoon I steered the tow out the harbor and up the lower part of the river. The current was ebbing so I was playing the current the whole time; keeping tight over by the Statue coming out of the Kills then across the channel to hug the Manhattan pierhead line all the way to the GW Bridge and then it was right up close against the east bank of the river, taking advantage of the lesser current there and riding ahead on the eddies in every cove and behind each point. In many places the water is deep right up to the shore, and it's possible to navigate within a stone's throw of the bank. In other spots there are submerged rocks, the remains of old piers, or ancient wrecks so if you're going to try to play the eddies you need to know where you're at. If you get in close enough you can cancel out most of the current and save a lot of distance compared to if you just sat out in mid-stream and bucked the current for six hours.

***

We slipped past the old Anaconda Copper plant at Hastings. A flat roofed, one story brick building spread across acres of river front long abandoned and then, recently, taken over by a demolition company to store debris. The new owners had packed the building, floor to ceiling, so that every cubic inch of it was solid with garbage and construction debris. The windows, the walls, and even the roof itself had herniated outward with eruptions of moldering waste. It was alarming, like a very bad dream; the big wire glazed industrial windows bulging ruptured in their frames and, inside, an infinite gray matter of chaos. It had become some kind of a super fund site, and yellow police tape fluttered all around it.

"For years I've been watching that building fill up with garbage and wondered how they were getting away with it. You or I throw a coffee cup out the window we get pulled over while they pay somebody to do that," Trevor said.

With that I handed the watch over to Trevor. He asked if it was alright if he kept out in the buoyed channel rather than hugging the shore as I had been doing. The ebb current that had been running all afternoon was about spent, and with the beginnings of the flood it was time to move out into the middle of the river anyway; but, still, I was glad that he asked. He also asked if I had the chart for the lower part of the river, and I got it out of the chart drawer for him. I wanted to be able to sleep on my time off and was pleased that Trevor was serious about knowing where he was. Del came up into the pilot house right at 1800, and I left the two of them there while I went down into the engine room to do a few chores: check the lube oil level in the engine, check the fuel filter gauges, check the temperature of all of the propeller shaft bearings, check the bilges. Then it was time to switch on the running lights for the night and go up on deck to check that all the bulbs were good. Then, figuring that we were going to need some heat on the boat overnight, I started up the furnace and hung around in the engine room, tidying up, until the boiler had gone through one cycle of getting up to normal pressure then shutting itself off. That done, I went through the watertight door that connected the engine room to the forecastle to check that the radiators were properly hot. Del was just finishing heating up a pot of rice and lamb that I had brought from home and he had set the forecastle table. I went up to the pilothouse to steer while Trevor and Del sat down to eat. We were in the top part of Haverstraw Bay with Stony Point and Verplanck up ahead.

"There's a down bound ship up by Bear Mountain and a gravel tow making up in behind Stony Point in Tompkins Cove. He probably won't get out of there before you're past him. I spoke to the ship and they'll be looking for you someplace between Verplanck and Indian Point," Trevor told me.

"Ok, go eat and thanks."

"You eat yet?" he asked.

"No, I'll eat when you come back up."

"I'm happy to sit up here if you want to go first."

"No, you go ahead." I liked doing it this way because the guy on watch was likely to eat quicker and get back up to the pilothouse if he knew somebody was up there in the dark waiting to eat.

It was fully dark by now. The air was chilly and clear with only a light breeze from the northwest. The surface of the river was ruffled just enough to make it impenetrably black, while the shore lights glared hard and bright. Glancing around the pilothouse I found that Trevor had adjusted all of the lights just right. The radar screen glowed faintly but its phosphorescent patches and dots were still fully readable. The engine gauges, the compass, chart plotter, depth sounder, and the GPS were all dimmed just the right amount so as not to interfere with the view ahead but were, at the same time, instantly readable when needed. The fair current swept us past Verplanck, the old steamboat wharf, the parking lot and the dimly lit neon of the ancient saloon that lingered there. The pilot of the downbound ship called again, announcing himself on the approach to the blind right turn at Jones Point.

"Security, security, the ship GYPSUM KING, southbound approaching Jones Point. GYPSUM KING approaching Jones Point to any concerned traffic."

I caught the microphone that hung from the overhead by my right shoulder, keyed it and called back, "Tug SPUYTEN DUYVIL, back to the GYPSUM KING."

"GYPSUM KING."

"Good evening cap'n. This is the tug SPUYTEN DUYVIL. We are northbound at Verplanck pushing a small barge. I wonder if you could pass us on a slow bell once you get around the point. We'll be well over on the east bank and will see you on one whistle."

"GYPSUM KING back to the SPUYTEN DUYVIL. One whistle and a slow bell, cap'n Thanks for coming in."

Then, another voice over the radio.

"McCormick Boys calling the southbound ship at Jones Point."

"GYPSUM KING back."

"Evening, Cap. We're just finished making up a southbound tow here in Tompkins Cove and will hold up 'til you get past. Over."

"GYPSUM KING back to the McCormack Boys. Thanks for holding up, Captain. We're cutting back to a slow bell passing the upbound tow at Verplanck but we'll be out of your way pretty quick. Thanks for coming back. GYPSUM KING, out."

The ship was a regular in and out of the river, hauling coral sand from the Bahamas to the cement plant at Cementon, famous for its cement. The ship's bow light appeared from behind the rocky head of Jones Point, then her high masthead light and below it, the dimmer green side light. Already the ship was deep into its right hand turn and as it swept around the point the bow and masthead lights closed up to stand one above the other and the other side light, red, blinked into view to share the aspect with the green light, until it was obscured by the continuing turn to leave the red side light only and the two white lights above separating now as the ship settled on its new course. It's always grand to watch a big ship make a turn in a narrow channel like that – so long as you don't end up right in front of it. I could see the point at which the pilot cut back his throttle as soon as he had completed the turn and the ship began to glide down to slow ahead in preparation for our passing.

The ship swept past and a minute or two later its wake reached us and caused the tug, the barge, and the heavy wires that connected us to wrench and squeal. A little water sloshed up onto the deck of the barge but none made it over the hatch coming into the hold.

"Everything OK?" Trevor asked, climbing up from the galley into the pilothouse.

"Oh yeah, It's just the Gypsum King going by."

"Well, I guess I can take it back from you. Peekskill light up there I see, Jones Point, and the light on Buoy 27," he said, picking off the steering marks ahead.

"You got it," I said. "I'm going to get dinner and then sleep a little. Del knows where things are. You call me if there's anything you're not sure about."

"OK. I shouldn't have anything to worry about with Del to show me where the switches and all are. You want me to wake you at midnight or do you want to sleep a bit longer?"

"No thanks, I'll be up at midnight. You got it 'til then."

I went down into the forecastle to get dinner which Del had set out on the table. He was washing dishes at the sink.

"This guy Trevor seems to know what he's doing," Del said over his shoulder.

"Yeah, I think he does. I think maybe we got lucky this time."

I wolfed down my meal, gave my empty dish to Del, still at the sink, and took one last look through the engine room, checking all of the same items as last time, and everything was normal. From the engine room I climbed the stair up to the stern deck into the chill valley air. Starting there and working forward I checked to see that all the lights were burning, amber and white shining brightly astern the green and red sidelights, port and starboard, the two white forward towing lights. Then I climbed out over the bow of the tug onto the barge and made my way forward to where red and green sidelights also burned and set between them on the bow of the barge, the amber flashing light which signified to all approaching that this was a barge being pushed. Out on the bow of the barge the unending racket of the tug's engine was only a low drumbeat and the reigning sound was the pillowing murmur of the river sloughing away around the bow. Overhead there were stars but no moon. The river banks were high and dark. The air was rich with an estuarine musk. Looking back, the little tug labored mightily, fumed and trembled in the halo of its running lights, radar turning with cardiac regularity, and a sooty jet of exhaust blasting straight up into the sky. I retrieved my flashlight from my back pocket and shone it down into the hold of the barge. The great machine sleeping there under its blue shroud almost filled the space. Everything looked to be in place and there was no sign of water anywhere down there. I made my way back onto the tug and passed one last time through the pilothouse. The clock there read just a little before 2200.

"Don't forget to call me if you need anything at all."

"Don't worry. I got it."

"Good night," I said and went down into the forecastle. I brushed my teeth, stuffed toilet paper in my ears to damp out the engine noise, kicked off my boots, and climbed fully clothed into my bunk, pulled the blanket over my head and slept as the tug pushed on up the old dark river.

***

Just before midnight, I was awake again. I listened to the sounds of the boat for a little to judge if everything was running right. Satisfied, I roll out of the bunk, step into my shoes, and go back to check the engine room. It is hot, bright, and loud; just like it ought to be. The first thing you do when you enter an engine room is smell the air. If there's anything wrong – diesel fuel, lube oil, hydraulic oil, or coolant leaking anywhere, or something getting too hot. Each little problem has its own smell and you will detect it right away, long before you would ever see it. On this night everything smelled fine; and I passed on through the engine room and up the stairs to the stern deck. Out there it was chilly and dark. Looking astern, I saw the looming mass of the Highlands and the lights of West Point tucked down in their little fold by the shore. Off to starboard and a little astern slept the haunted ruin of Bannerman's Island and I was glad to see that we had made it up through the narrow part of the river where it passes through the Highlands and where the current, now setting up against us for the next six hours, runs far stronger than it will in the broad expanse of river that lies for the next few miles ahead. There are a number of bottlenecks where if you get caught with a heavy tow and a contrary current, you're not going anywhere for the next six hours, and it can really make a mess of all your careful bidding on a job. West Point, Hell Gate, The Race, the Cape Cod or the C&D Canal; each of these can cost you six long hours of full wages and sleep if you're not careful.

"Hey, you made it through the Highlands. I wasn't so sure we were going to make it," I said as greeting when I came into the pilothouse.

"I tell you," Trevor's voice came out of the dim light, "I was beginning to have my doubts back there coming through World's End I thought we'd lost the current but then it seemed to hold off just enough to get us up to Cold Spring and now we're in the clear."

"Well, you got us through the narrow part anyway, so I guess I can take her for a while. You all get some sleep."

Del was standing by the door at the other side of the pilothouse and asked if I needed anything before he and Trevor went down.

"Yeah, pass me up a Coke if you would," which he did while Trevor briefed me on our position and on whatever traffic might be moving within radio range. At the moment there was none.

"Thank you," I told him. "I'll give you a shout just before six."

"You can wake me before that if you get tired."

"Thanks, I'll be fine." And with that I was left alone.

It took a few minutes to set up the pilothouse the way I wanted it. First off, Trevor had fogged up the windows with his smoking. I opened the doors and side windows to air the place out while I took a paper towel and Windex to the front glass. The cold night air flooded into the space and purged the last of my sleepiness. A few minutes later, sitting in the helmsman's chair behind perfectly transparent glass, with the radar and all of the other lights dimmed to the bare minimum, my can of Coke lodged in its holder by the wheel, I settled into my watch.

It is a nice clear night with just enough breeze to keep the river fog from setting in. Around two o'clock a speedboat rockets past, headed downstream on some antic mission of pleasure or vice; and twice the radio crackles with the communication of some vessel at work far out just beyond the radio's range up here among the river hills. The fact that the signal is no stronger the second time suggests that the voice is also bound upriver and traveling at about the same speed as I am. I steer on up the river, facing the bright shore lights of Newburgh, then coast along the shore lined up for the Newburgh Bridge, then steer wide of the glaring lights of the power plant on Danskammer Pt. until I pick up the lighted buoy on the Middle Ground just off Wappingers Creek. Along the west shore there are vineyards and the rich smell of ripened grapes fills the river valley for a time during the long straight approach to the Poughkeepsie Bridge and Crum Elbow beyond and we are just past the Elbow and moving into the Long Reach when the first light is beginning to outline the contour of the eastern hilltops and the ebb current is dropping off, getting ready to go slack and then run fair again. The hour hand finally gets to six and I can hear Trevor and Del moving around down below and it's their turn to get up and steer.

Ten minutes later Trevor is up in the pilothouse. I fill him in on what's been happening which is basically nothing, take a brief tour through the engine room where everything is running fine and go quickly to my bunk, shed everything except my undershorts, and lie down; hurrying to get my eyes closed before the daylight gets into them to wake me up for the rest of the day. I fall into a deep and peaceful sleep as soon as my head hits the pillow. The satisfaction of having completed those long dark hours and to have turned the helm over to the daylight and to the next man affords me a satisfying slumber.

A little after 0900 I am awake, feeling pretty new. Daylight filters down through the forecastle skylight. The engine hammers along at its accustomed beat. I roll my legs out of the bunk and sit up with my feet on the steel deck. Across the way, Del sits at the galley table carefully reading a day old copy of the Enquirer. I pull on my clothes and look around on the galley counter for something to eat. The coffee maker still holds a couple of cups and there's a box of Entenmann's pastry lying open, half gone.

"Anybody got dibs on this coffee?" I ask Del.

"No, Cap'n, it's all yours."

With my breakfast I sit down at the table.

Del seriously looks up from his paper. "Sleep OK?" he asked.

"Yes! It was great. How are you guys doing?"

"V-Very good. We're just past S-S-Saugerties." He had a stammer and I always admired the way he would tackle words like that head-on.

"How're you and Trevor getting along?"

Del's face brightens, "Fine. H-he really knows the river."

Del could be moody and his feelings easily hurt so to hear an unqualified response was good news.

"H-he's a funny guy," Del adds with a chuckle and the rest of my breakfast passes in silence as Del returns to his study of the tabloid.

By the time I finish eating and carefully check through the engine room and all around the deck, Del is sitting with Trevor up in the pilothouse.

"You gotta see this," Del said as I came in.

The two of them are looking at something with a conspiratorial air which Trevor breaks away from every few seconds to check the river ahead. Leering just a little, Trevor hands me a color snapshot. It shows a bell buoy, green with the number 27 stuck to it in reflective plastic. Within the pyramid lattice of its superstructure hangs the usual large, bronze-green bell. The buoy occupies the near field in calm water and behind it, across the water, out of focus but still identifiable is the Indian Point Nuclear power plant, right back where we were last night when the Gypsum King sailed past. The snapshot, however, was obviously taken in daytime from a boat stationed near the buoy and, as is the case with most snapshots taken from boats, the whole image is kiltered so that the horizon is off and the buoy appears to be on the verge of tipping over even though the river surface is barely ruffled. But even if, as a composition, the picture has little to offer, as a story it is howling for a narrative, because standing on the deck of the buoy, legs spread wide for balance, one arm extended to hold the bell tower frame and the other extended in a high, proud salute, is a naked woman, sleek as a seal, brown as a bean, big breasted, dark nippled, full bodied but unrippled, handsome, maybe five foot two, short haired, and gleeful.

"I never seen a seal that far up-river," I remarked and Trevor and Del laughed. "Where in God's name did you get that?"

"I took it myself!" said Trevor proudly. "That pretty little gal's named Flo, Florence Izquerdo. Pretty nice, huh? And, she's also a certified welder!"

"Wow," I replied.

"All last summer, on each of my two weeks off, I ran the work boat on a job they were doing rebuilding the cooling water outfall at Indian Point. Flo was one of the welders on the job and we got to be friends. She used to ride on the boat with me when she wasn't welding. I decided that I'd try to get her to pose on that buoy with no clothes on. It took most of the summer to talk her into it, but, as you can see…."

"I can see; but, why?"

"I don't know. A challenge I guess."

"Were you, like, having a thing?"

"Oh, no! Not on your life. She had a boyfriend who every day dropped her off and picked her up at work. Guy about 6'4" with pictures shaved into the side of his head for Christ sake! No way − I'm not touching that."

"But what if he found out about it?"

"Oh, she gave him a copy," he said, which struck me as a kind of a rash move.

***

A little before my watch began at noon I walked around the boat once again to check on things, looking in the bilges and into all the dark corners below deck. After that I went all around on deck and finally up onto the barge and while I was up there, looking down into the deep hold which held our cargo, I saw a herring gull standing on one of the timber sleepers on which the generator was set. Down at the bottom of the hold, surrounded by the 12 foot walls of the barge and crowded by the bulk of the huge machine with which it shared the space, the bird looked tiny and frail, though gulls in their normal surroundings are usually able to maintain a more arrogant pose. It wasn't too hard to guess how the bird had gotten down there. They sleep on the water at night, and it's not unusual for a barge being pushed to sneak up on them. When surprised like that they will sometimes hop up into the air right in front of the barge just high enough to re-land immediately on its deck. Perhaps, in the darkness, this bird had dropped back down, not onto the short front deck of the barge, but had sailed a little farther back and fluttered into the hold where the narrow confines had trapped it.

Gulls get themselves into all sorts of difficulties and most of those have to do with appetite. For example, there used to be a barge moored back behind Staten Island, not far from the Fresh Kills garbage dump, on which swarms of gulls used to roost and to which they used to carry bones found in the dump. The deck of the barge was strewn with these bits of carrion and because the hatches of the barge were left open for ventilation some of these tidbits would inevitably fall down into the interior of the barge and then a greedy gull would venture itself down the hatch after the bone, and it would be unable to fly back out. Down there it would begin a slow death from either starvation or thirst. Perhaps because it would cry out occasionally or because once dead it attracted other gulls by its own decay, more birds would venture down through the hatch until in the course of months there would be a heap of birds piled below the hatch. Once, late at night, I peered into that barge and in the beam of my flashlight witnessed a snarled mass of dead and dying gulls, while off in the nearby recesses, standing wraithlike in the oblique shadows of the flashlight beam, another few birds stood dejected. It was not my problem. There was nothing to be done. I went on my way.

This time, I climbed down into the hold, and the lone gull eyed me sharply. As I approached, it half unfolded its wings and fluttered back against the steel. I drove it to the corner of the hold and trapped it there with my legs while I wrestled to get a hold on its wings. It bit my wrist again and again with fierce jabs of its beak until I finally had it under control, pinned beneath my arm with its head behind me where all its beak could do was drum against the brown canvas of my jacket. I climbed back up the ladder one handed and regaining the deck of the barge, flung the bird over the side. It tumbled in the air as it spread its wings, stabilized almost instantly and glided maybe 20 yards to land on the river. It turned to watch the tug as it moved on, then fluffed its feathers and solemnly began to preen as if nothing had happened.

When I stepped back into the pilothouse Trevor and Del were laughing.

"I saw you coming up the ladder with that thing under your arm, I thought maybe we were going to have it for lunch," Trevor said. "How'd you get ahold of it without it biting you?"

"It did bite me," I replied.

"I tell you, if it had been me, I'd have kicked it first. Those things are vicious. A guy once told me they're made of piss."

"It had enough troubles without me kicking it," I said.

"I used to work on the garbage run with a guy who would sit his whole watch with a little .22 pump on his lap. He'd steer with his feet, keep one window open and shoot every gull that landed on the pile of garbage out in front of him. He'd go through a couple boxes of shells every watch. He kept at it until one day, going through the Kills, he accidentally put a hole in the pilothouse window of a Moran tug coming the other way. There was union trouble going on at the time so the Coast Guard got involved and it got in the papers. He didn't get caught but he decided not to do that anymore."

It was noon. We were just passing under the Rip Van Winkle Bridge as I took over steering and started the long swing around the bend to line up with Hudson Light. We still had a bit of fair current running with us and to make the most of it, I chose to take the passage along the west bank of the river past the town of Athens rather than keep to the buoyed route on the east past the town of Hudson. Until the river was finally dredged out in 1918 to create a deep water passage all the way to Albany, the Athens side had been the main channel. Still, there's good enough depth through there for smaller vessels and it cuts a little distance off the trip.

"Jeez, I haven't been through here for thirty years at least," Trevor said. "I think most of the companies would fire any captain on the spot if they went this way."

"It used to be the only way to go and I've been told it's no different now than it was then. In fact, first boat I worked on up here the captain wouldn't let you go through by the town of Hudson."

Though it was once a busy riverfront town there's almost nothing left of Athens anymore, but just past the town there's a hollowed out basin which long ago was a shipyard and now is a ship graveyard, with a couple of old wooden tugs, a floating crane and a few other unidentifiable hulks – all sunk.

"That's Ray Phelps' old place," I said. "All that stuff used to be his and it actually used to float. He and I worked together on a dredging job for Warren Disch a bunch of years back. He was in his eighties then but still probably the biggest guy I've ever met. Scary big, but just a sweetheart behind it all."

"I never met him," Trevor said.

"He was one of those guys who came up in the harbor before the war and just kinda learned how to do everything. He'd go towing, or dock building, or dredging or even fishing. He had a little tug that he took out to Shinnecock and converted it over into a dragger and then when the fishing got bad, he switched it back into a tug again. I understand he switched it back and forth over and over."

"That was before everything had to have a license and it was easier to do whatever you wanted," Trevor observed. "Freedom or free doom."

"Yah, I guess old Ray kinda had it both ways. One time, back there in his yard, he was down in the engine room trying to get a broken valve spring out of one of the heads on his engine. He had the head resting on blocks on the engine room floor and he had his hand under it trying to poke the spring up out of it when it tipped off the blocks and pinned his hand. He was down there on the engine room floor for three days until his friends up at the bar started asking each other, 'Hey, whatever happened to old Ray?' and somebody went down to look for him."

"That's what happens when you're working alone. Not a good thing."

"Speaking of working alone, I guess it's my watch now. I'm thinking we'll make it up to Troy tonight maybe around eight o'clock and then we'll go straight up through the Federal Lock and tie up for the rest of the night below lock two. That way we can get some decent sleep and start into the canal first thing tomorrow."

"Fine with me," Trevor said. "Years ago, going right by Troy at eight o'clock at night was something you just didn't do. Just when the saloons and the whore houses were getting lit up."

"I don't know there's much of that available in Troy anymore," I said.

"Oh, probably not," Trevor said. "You always have the chance to stop on the way back. If there's nothing you need me to do, I'm going to lie down for a while."

"Go right ahead. I'll give you or Del a shout if I need anything."

***

Just above the towns of Athens and Hudson, the river changes. The banks are lower and more overgrown with cottonwood and willow. The stream braids into side channels and low islands and there is more and more evidence of the work that has been done to improve the river channel. Increasingly the shore is reinforced with timber bulkheads to control the river current, to direct it into each bend, to help to scour out the passage. Above Athens, it is obviously not a wild river anymore as you might imagine it to be lower down. All along the banks there are the vestiges of human activity, ruined wharves, old piles of quarried stone that no one ever came to float away. For long stretches, the shore of the river is red with the debris of former brickyards; broken, misfired, or just abandoned brick pushed over the bank to build out the shore in disorderly swales. Here and there, like the columns of an ancient civilization lost in the jungle still stand long abandoned brickyard chimneys, elaborately corbelled, flared, tapered, and tumbled to advertise the counterintuitive fluency of a brick in the hands of the right bricklayer.

It was a beautiful afternoon. It was clear and sunny and it became warm and still. The yellowing leaves along the shore lit up the water. I rode with the pilothouse windows down and the mellow air drifted through. We passed Coxsackie, New Baltimore, and Coeymans. Just below Roah Hook a tug with a big oil barge on a short towline passed; bound down from Albany. The tug looked gallant as it approached framed by the looming bow of the barge close behind it. As it came around the river bend the bow of the barge swept grandly out beside the tug, rolled the tug just noticeably as the strain came on the tow wire, then the barge swung back obediently astern and the tug rolled placidly back to plumb. We didn't bother to speak to one another on the radio as there was no danger of confusion even though the river width was only a fraction of what it had been the day before. At night, in snow, or fog, the passing would have been tense, careful, and the language passed back and forth on the radio, clipped; but here and now it was perfectly simple.

Later in the afternoon we began to prepare the tug and tow for entering the canal. The low bridges that we would encounter there required that we reduce the overhead clearance of the tug as much as possible. This meant folding down the mast which carried the tug's towing lights, and unbolting the radar antenna from its mounting on the pilothouse roof, wrapping it in a plastic tarp and lashing it down on its side. On the bow of the barge a searchlight was rigged with light lines running back into the pilothouse so that the helmsman would be able to train it left and right, traveling at night on the narrow canal.

By six that evening we were past the Selkirk Bridge and as darkness came on, the glow of the Port of Albany with its deepwater piers, warehouses, and tank farms was plain ahead. By 7:30 we were through the railroad bridge just above Albany and in half an hour more, close enough to Troy to reach the Federal Lock by radio to notify them of our approach. They would have the lock ready for us when we arrived. We pushed on through Troy and right around the next bend came upon the dam and tucked into the east bank, the Federal Lock. With Trevor steering, Del and I went up onto the barge as we nosed into the lock chamber and put out lines next to the lock keeper's office. I went back to the pilothouse to get the boat's papers, then climbed up onto the lock wall and went into the office to sign in.

"Where you taking that?" the lock keeper asked. "And what is it?" as he peered out the window into the glare of the sodium lights that blazed over the lock.

"It's a generator going to Syracuse. Siemens product, all the way from Germany."

"What's the matter with a GE product? They make them right here."

"This one's better, I guess."

"I suppose it is," the lock keeper replied. He finished up with the paperwork, while the water level in the lock slowly rose, lifting the tug and barge from sea level to the height of the river above the dam. "You're all set. I guess you know, when you come out of the lock chamber you steer to the right and get as far away as you can from the left hand wall or else the current will hold you up against it all the way out and you can get into trouble. Water's low right now – only three feet over the dam - so there's not so much of a problem, but it's good practice anyway."

"Thanks," I told him. "I've seen it up here when it's really running and I know to look out for it."

"That's good," he replied. "You only need to see it running high one time to get the message."

The lock is tucked into the right-hand bank of the river and alongside it is the dam which establishes the difference in river levels below and above the lock which in normal conditions is 14 feet with two or three feet of water depth falling over the lip of the dam. But during the spring run-off or whenever there has been an unusual downpour of rain the river can rise into a brown torrent with better than 10 feet roaring over the dam and creating islands of foam which drift for miles downstream in the current, a warning to any tug bound into the canal that conditions at the Federal Lock will be difficult. And the principal difficulty there lies in the character of the long thin jetty that extends out from the upstream opening of the lock, separating the exit channel of the lock from the main body of the river. Called a lead-out wall, it invites the helmsman of a tug pushing a barge to guide himself close along the face of the wall until reaching the open river about 400 feet ahead. But this is not a normal wall because below the water surface the wall is only resting on widely spaced pilings which allow the river current to flow downstream through the exit channel, then out under the wall. This constant flow will hold an exiting barge against the wall for no reason that is apparent to the helmsman. He will steer the barge away from the wall, but probably not sharply enough to counter the force holding him and, so, will slide the length of the wall, trying to figure out what is happening, perhaps even increasing throttle to provide more steering power, until, reaching the end of the wall the full river current will catch the front of the barge, jack-knife it around the end of the wall and carry it away toward the dam. At the point the barge jack-knifes around the end of the wall its wire and rope connections to the tug pushing it will probably break, saving the tug from a trip over the dam; and the barge, if it is loaded deep enough will not actually go over the dam either as it will ground out on the sill. Even so, it is a nightmarish scenario, and serves as a reminder that, for a boatman, every place has its own peculiarities.

Trevor brought the tug and tow out of the lock perfectly, keeping well away from the wall from the very start; and, in another half an hour, we were tying up below the first lock of the Erie Canal. It was just about 11 and we had until 7 a.m. to wait until the canal reopened in the morning. I went down into the engine room and shut down the engine and the generator. The tug's batteries would provide what few lights we would need for the night. For the first time in a day and a half it was quiet.

***

"First summer I ever worked up here," Trevor said as we sat around the galley table finishing breakfast, "was on a boat called the Arrow. We were mostly moving oil up to Rome and it was just these two old Norwegians, captain and engineer, and me, the kid; and those two were thick as thieves, like two old queens all the time bickering and telling stories to each other in Norwegian and they treated me like their slave. Every night they'd tie up someplace close to a bar and go up the street together leaving me to watch the boat. Then sometime after midnight they'd come back drunk, crash around for a while, swearing and knocking things over then fall asleep and I'd have to wake 'em up in the morning with eggs and bacon, coffee, toast – a whole spread. Each of 'em every night would put his false teeth in a cup on the floor by his bunk before he went to sleep and one morning toward the end of the season when I couldn't stand it anymore I switched their teeth around. They sat there at the table, hung over, kinda working their gums trying to figure out what was going on and after a while they kind of sheepishly reach into their mouths and trade teeth. I was expecting they'd come after me but they never figured it out so I did it every now and then for the rest of the season and every time they would just kinda look at one another, sort of nod and grunt like Norwegians used to do, and switch teeth."

I climbed ashore and hiked up the long flight of concrete steps that led up to the lock to check in. I got to the shack just as the lock tender was climbing out of his car. Everything was damp and dripping from the fog that had settled into the river valley during the small hours of the morning. But overhead there was already a wash of blue sky showing and it promised to be another warm, calm day.

"Let's hope this weather gets you all the way to Syracuse and back," the tender said. "It's getting kind of late in the year. I think you'll be the last tow coming back out this season and they're planning to close the system down behind you as you come back out."

"Well, let's hope the weather stays nice, for everybody's sake."

"Like I said, it's too late in the year to stay nice for long."

Once I had filled out the paperwork I walked back down to the tug. Trevor was standing on deck with Del.

"You want me and Del to handle lines?" he asked.

"No, why don't you run it? It's your watch. Del and I will do the decking up through the flight."

The first five locks of the Erie Canal climb almost 170 feet in the space of a mile and a half, skirting around the Falls of the Mohawk River where it drops into the Hudson. The close succession of locks is called The Flight because of its resemblance to a flight of stairs, the locks being so closely spaced and regular in dimension. Each is a rectangular concrete box, 300 feet long and 43.5 feet wide; each end is fitted with a double doored gate which is slightly wider than the width of the lock chamber so that when the gate is closed it forms a shallow "V" angled against the water pressure that it will have to withstand as the lock is filled or drained. This pressure forces the doors of the gate tight against each other to form a watertight seal. Water to fill or to drain the lock chamber is piped in and out through valves set low down in the chamber walls so that the rise and fall of the water level can be accomplished with a minimum of turbulence. Nowhere in the entire length of the Erie Canal is water mechanically pumped to or from a lock. Throughout the system water is supplied by gravity, collected from a source above the lock and delivered by natural streams, by channels, sluices or by the course of the canal itself to the locks at lower elevation. The first section of the canal, the Flight, is a detour around the set of falls over which the Mohawk River tumbles into the Hudson. After this obstacle is passed and for the next 115 miles westward the canal route follows the course of the Mohawk, all the way to Rome. Most of the canal length in this section runs in a dredged channel of the river itself, the current and level of which is managed by a series of dams alongside each of which is a lock to lift a vessel into the level beyond. In a few of these river sections, such as at Little Falls, there are rapids to be bypassed; and the canal diverts into a manmade channel and a series of locks remote from the river; but as soon as practicable the canal rejoins the river's natural, though much altered, bed.

Del and I cast off the lines, securing the barge at the seawall below the first lock, as Trevor clutches the tug ahead. At dead slow speed we push into the lock. The walls rise 35 feet on each side of us. They are slick with a thin brown algae, while the water surface is sprinkled with bits of green duckweed and bright autumn leaves.

Del and I stand at the forward corners of the barge, ready to use the looped ends of our docking lines as fenders between the barge and the lock walls should Trevor scuff them on the way in. But he brings the barge into the lock without touching either side and pushes right on to the very front of the lock where there is a set of mooring pins mounted into recesses in the lock wall. Up the height of the wall there are two of these pins; the first at ten feet above the water, the second at 20 feet and then at the top of the lock wall where it gives out onto a concrete walkway, set back from the edge of the wall by about five feet, there is a steel mooring post about a foot tall and mushroom shaped. From down below in the empty lock chamber this last post is well out of sight, but its location is marked by a yellow arrow painted at the very top of the wall. On the bow of the barge Del and I put our docking lines onto the lowest of the mooring pins to hold the tug and barge in place while the lock tender up on the top of the wall throws the switches that close the downstream lock gates right behind us. Then the lock tender walks up to the upstream end of the lock and throws the switch to open the valves that will fill the lock. The water level begins to rise with only the slightest surge to and fro of the tug and barge. Soon, we have risen a third of the way up the chamber wall and Del and I slip our lines off the lower mooring pin and toss them onto the one above it. We hold them there until the barge has risen some more, and then we take off the lines and toss the eye spliced ends of our lines to catch the mooring post set back from the top of the wall.

On this occasion, Del and I both miss our first throws. My second connects. It is always this way for us at the beginning of a canal passage, being out of practice; but deckhands that work in the canal full time develop an unerring skill at tossing lines up and over the corner of the walls.

"Little rusty there, Cap," Del chides me. "Gotta sharpen up."

"Practice, practice, practice."

"Trevor was saying how he was worried you were going to make him deck up through the Flight. He said it's been twenty years since he's done it."

"Oh, I wouldn't do that to him, too much fun," I said. "How are you and Trevor getting along?"

"He's a hot shit!" said Del with a lot more enthusiasm than usual. "And he really knows what he's doing."

We rose up out of the depths of the lock until we had a view of the still reflective pool of the canal ahead and to either side of us, the neatly manicured lawn and plantings around the lock and the little lock tender's house, white stucco with strong blue and orange trim. The gate ahead of us relaxes as the water level on both sides equalizes and a thin seam of light appears at the opening. Then, hydraulic motors whistle into action and the doors begin to surge open. In a moment they are swung into their pockets on the lock walls and we are free to move ahead to the next lock. We throw off the lines as Trevor sets the tug in motion.

In less than two hours we are past the Flight and on our way up the Mohawk. There's a point in the Flight, when you are in Lock number six after it is filled, that you can look back down into the valley behind and you get a sudden sense of the genius of the canal to magically transport the heaviest things uphill. Down the hillside behind you tumble the rooftops and tree tops of an inland village. A smokestack and a factory stand tiny below, while a tugboat, a barge, a brand new machine, and three men rise up and up into the countryside, bound into the continent.

"Welcome to the sponge," Trevor said as he slowly ramped up the throttle out of the last lock and started into the long marshy turn leading to the low bridge at Crescent. "That's all this is, you know; just one vast sponge."

***

Now, as we pushed up through the long slow bends in the river between Scotia and Rotterdam, I asked Trevor, "How are you and Del getting along?"

"Oh, he's fine." Trevor replied. "I've been dying to ask where you found him. He's like something out of central casting. Right down to the name, Delbert Flynn! I haven't run into a deckhand like him for at least 20 years!"

"How do you mean?" I asked.

"I mean he's just so, you know; *basic*, I guess. I mean he's just *there*. Doesn't seem to get tired, doesn't seem to eat. Doesn't talk much. Just sits there studying the *Enquirer* until you give him something to do. He's even got the smelly feet!"

"Yeah, the feet are a problem. I've found the trick is to try to make sure he keeps his boots on. If he takes them off it's bad so whenever he does I invent something for him to do on deck like checking the running lights or something and that gets the boots back on until the next time."

"Don't complain. A deckhand like yours is worth his weight in gold. You wouldn't believe some of the guys I have to work with. Can't even get 'em out of their bunk and then first thing they do is start bitching and moaning, and then they get themselves hurt. You know, looking back at it, the best guy I ever had was a deaf mute. Watched what was going on like a hawk, learned quicker than you would believe, and, of course, never said nothing."

"Sounds perfect," I said.

"Pretty much," Trevor continued, "except one time he was up on the barge setting up the push wires and he lost most of the fingers on his right hand. I saw it coming from the pilothouse and yelled my head off; but, of course, him not hearing, it didn't do any good."

"I've never hurt anybody on here, thank God," I said, looking around for something made of wood.

"Well, you've just got to be alert every second of the day, and you've got to have people working for you who pay attention, too. And keeping it simple like you do helps a lot. You've got a nice little operation here. Seems like you've got just the right amount of everything which is a far cry from the way they do things on the bigger boats with six or eight people tripping over each other. I've always thought that this is what I'd like to end up doing. Just a small boat and a simple operation where you can keep control of things and have it the way you want it."

"I'm not sure you'll ever get it exactly the way you want but at least you always know who to complain to."

"I guess you must make pretty good money on a job like this," Trevor offered.

"Well," I was careful in answering this, "it depends. You've got to bid the job like everybody else and so you've got to shave it pretty close to the bone. You figure what you need to get per hour to make it work and then figure out as best you can how to do it in the least amount of time.

Then you just try to keep to the schedule. You do it the way you figured it, you come out alright, you do it quicker you make yourself some extra. You screw up, you lose. There's no going back to the customer and trying to fix it up after the fact – you'll just piss him off and probably lose him for good. So you learn to eat your mistakes."

"That's a lot different from what I do – work my hours and draw my check. I think I'd like it," Trevor said, a little sadly.

"I do, but it's not for everybody."

Trevor was a very good helmsman. In the river, with its wide bends, he always started into his turn well before each bend; edging out toward the middle of the channel as he approached the bend and then starting the barge swinging into the turn well before the point of land or buoy that he was going to pass. By beginning the turn well beforehand he would already be beginning to slow the turn of the barge by the time he had reached the buoy. In this way the tug and barge would settle right onto the new course up the channel ahead. Sitting in the pilothouse with him, as he eased the tow through the bends, I could tell that he had that natural boat handling skill which could not be taught, but was the product of instinct and many, many years of devotion. Often I had sat in this same position as a less skillful mate or deckhand wrestled the tug through a turn, using far too much rudder, fighting the forces with which he might just as easily be cooperating. Sometimes it was all I could do not to grab the wheel away and ease the tow back into shape. I had found that it was of little use to try to instruct anyone, but had reached the belief that good boat handling stemmed from some natural instinct for the dance of mass and motion which could not be taught and probably not even appreciated by the non-elect.

"You know," Trevor said as he looked keenly ahead, "this boat handles this barge pretty well for its size. I've seen a lot of smaller boats like this that would be dragged all over the place with this size of a load."

"It's a pretty heavy boat for its size, and I think it's got just about the right amount of power."

"I think you're right. There's people who would try to put twice the power into a boat like this and then would get all upset because it didn't handle right."

"I've got just a little under 600 horsepower in here and there's a boat just like this one where they decided to put in 1100 and first thing they did was capsize it and they got it back up and then capsized it again six months later. Then they decided it was no good and sold it to some guy in Norfolk who drowned himself in it."

"Less you really know what you're doing you don't want a lot of power, particularly in a smaller boat. Only get you in trouble."

"And cost you more in fuel," I said.

"That too," said Trevor.

We worked our way up the course of the Mohawk, past Schenectady, Amsterdam, and Tribes Hill. Most of the way, we shared the river valley with the Thruway on one side and the ConRail tracks on the other. On the Thruway east and westbound cars and trailer trucks flew past us while on the opposite bank the Conrail freight trains squealed and clicked their way with gondolas filled with coal, flatcars stacked with trailers, and boxcars carrying the insignia of every railroad on the continent. Huge amounts of cargo were on the move in the valley, and we were a part of it, churning along at a fast walk with our ponderous load: too big for either rail or trailer. We were headed into the lowering autumn sunlight as the afternoon wore on. The light shone in through the pilothouse windows. The space grew warm, so I opened the doors on both sides of the pilothouse to let in the Indian summer air. I was half way through my watch and Del and Trevor were asleep below taking advantage of the ten miles or so between Locks 13 and 14 – two hours to rest before the next locking through.

Earlier, over sandwiches that we had eaten in the pilothouse, Trevor had told a story about his early days on the canal. Working for Oil Transfer as mate aboard the HARBOR STAR running between New York and points all up and down the canal with heating oil and how, tied up one night westbound at Baldwinsville (pronounced, "Bollinsville") he had gone ashore to the bar there and met a farm girl, "Not so pretty," as he had described her, and had brought her back to his cabin on the tug. They had been "kinda drunk" he said and after they had screwed around for a while, she left. At dawn the tug got underway again and two days later they were on their way back through Baldwinsville with the empty barge. Trevor had not gone ashore this time but the engineer did and next morning told Trevor that there were two big farm boys looking for him and very upset about their sister and Trevor got worried but the engineer reassured Trevor that it would be OK. The girl, it turned out, had only a dim recollection of what had happened and somehow the wrong name for the tug had become stuck in her head. So, for the rest of that season on the canal the two brothers would show up occasionally at one lock or another looking for a tugboat called the HARVESTER.

109

"One time I actually leaned out of the pilothouse window while they stood on the edge of the lock, my face not four feet away from the name board with HARBOR STAR carved out in four inch gold leaf and told those two guys that I thought the HARVESTER would be along later in the week."

And so, we towed west through the bright afternoon. We took turns sleeping. The day had warmed up so that by mid-afternoon there were folks down along the canal bank, fishing; old guys just sitting with their bait and their poles on the leader walls and once in a while an outboard boat went by. Once, while Del was out on the barge setting up our searchlight for the night, a boat with one guy and two girls came up from behind, passed us cautiously, and then, once well in front of us one of the girls stood up in the boat and flipped up her shirt, not revealing much but still getting the point across. Del came back to the tug shaking his head in disbelief.

"Did you see that?" he asked.

"I did," Trevor replied. "You can always tell when you've made it into the back country when the girls start flashing you."

"I never quite understood why they do that," I said.

Trevor explained, "It's not personal to you in any way. It's just to stir up their dull boyfriends."

"Where do you figure to stop tonight?" Trevor asked. "There used to be a pretty good little road house right near Lock 14 at Canajoharie."

Del laughed.

"I wasn't figuring to stop unless we had to," I replied. "We usually keep going unless we get shut down by the river fog in the early morning and we should be up on the Rome level by then so we can just tie up to a tree if we have to."

"Oh well," Trevor said bravely, "That road house is probably long gone anyway. The State cops put 'em all out of business sitting just outside the parking lot and picking off the drunks as they drove out."

"I'm sure we'll get to stop someplace," I said. "It's just I'm figuring to have this thing in Syracuse by daylight Tuesday morning and that means we've got to keep pushing right along."

"I gotcha, Cap," said Trevor with a shade of irony.

Around dusk we arrived at Canajoharie and actually did tie up and shut down the engine for a little while just past the lock so that we could sit down to dinner and so that I could make a careful check of the engine before running on into the night. Del had warmed up a fish stew that I had brought from home. I had made it big enough so that it would feed three and then could stay warm on the back of the stove for the next day or so.

"This is the real thing!" Trevor announced as we sat around the table. "You make this? I haven't had anything like this since I was a kid up in New England."

"Well, that's just about where it's from. You get yourself a nice big cod's head; you put in a pot and boil it until it all falls apart, then throw in onion and potato and whatever salt and pepper; salt pork if you got any. You can also use bacon provided you cook it first."

"Where do you get a cod's head these days?" Trevor asked.

"You just walk through the Fulton Fish Market any time late at night. The fish cutting houses down there would lay a truckload on you if you wanted them. You cook it down until all the bones fall apart and then you fish them out from the bottom of the pot and maybe some of the skin but everything else is still in there. You find an eyeball you win the prize."

"And what prize is that?"

"Fish stew for breakfast?" I offered.

"The other eye," blurted Del.

We finish up the meal. I check through the engine room, check the running lights and we are on our way once more.

***

Trevor is sitting in the helmsman's chair with a wreath of cigarette smoke swirling around his face. It was just at the last edge of sunlight and the light pouring in low on his face revealed a texture of fine wrinkles. He looked older in this light, transparent, and somehow frail. He stared into the length of the canal ahead; his eyes squinted nearly shut against the bright. "You know," he began, " it was just about right here that I heard a story once, so seeing we're here right now too I might as well tell it to you. Mind you, it's got nothing to do with this actual place except for the fact that this is where I first heard it and, so, I've always figured if there are ghosts then that's what they are, just a story that gets attached to a place.

"It was one of the Dragon brothers, Tommy or Billy, I can't remember. There was one of them never washed and the other almost never washed. They were from up around Fort Edward, born on the canal back in the old horse and mule days and hung on into the sixties. One of them, when

113

he was a kid, worked for a dock builder up here. They would work non-stop all through the summer, living on a quarter barge that stayed with the dock building rig because most of the time their jobs were way the hell and gone in the middle of nowhere; and then at the end of the canal season the rig got tied up and they'd all get laid off, and that's the way it was done. But this one year the company got wind of a big steel car float sunk at the dock in Red Hook, Brooklyn. Nobody'd been able to raise it and they were offering a lot of money to anyone that could. So the company, who I guess maybe didn't even really know what a car float was because they're way too big to ever get up into the canal, decided that he would send the rig and crew down to New York to try to keep some work going through the winter. So the crane and the quarter barge got towed down to New York at the end of the season. Now, in the crew there was a French Canadian who used to sneak back and forth across the border to work for the company each season and was called, as you might expect, the Canuck. He was a handy guy, hard worker, didn't speak much English, but his real selling point was that he had this old Ford pick-up which was useful for work sometimes but extra useful getting from wherever the quarter barge happened to be tied up to the nearest bar. So even though there might have been some customs and immigration complications with the Canuck's tagging along – and those things weren't all that tough back in those days – he was invited to come along anyway sort of by popular demand.

"They got down there and pretty quick found out that sunken car floats are a bitch to get up; and the winter turned out to be a ball buster and everything they did went wrong and finally, in the middle of one bitter cold night – they were working it as a tide job as they could get at the deck only at low tide – the Canuck fell down through an open hatch when nobody was looking and drowned. It was a good hour before they managed to get him out and once they had him laid out on the dock in the snow they realized that they had been so busy trying to get him out that nobody had thought to call the cops or anything and who would you call anyway back then except to make trouble, and a little after that they realized that they didn't really even know who the guy was except he was the Canuck and not supposed to be there in the first place, so they decided that the best thing to do was to just return him to Canada soon as they had a chance. So they laid him out in the bed of the truck, iced him up good with snow, and then it was just getting light and they were all cold and hungry, so they all piled in and drove up to the bar to get a drink and a breakfast, and that developed into a sort of a wake and by the time that wound down they were all tired, and so they went back down to the quarter barge to catch a nap before the afternoon low tide.

"Their intentions were good, but those low tides just kept coming every twelve hours, another long cold shift, another trip to the bar for a drink and a sandwich, another nap, and so on. Fact is, nobody wanted to be the one to take the truck and the Canuck back over the border, and the truck was their only means of getting to and from the bar and the weather was staying perfectly cold; so they just kept working on the salvage job while keeping a good pile of snow in the back of the truck, figuring that when the job was done they would have time to figure out how to get the Canuck back to his people up north, even though none of them was even sure that he had any people. And then they started seeing that the season was changing and not so cold and the snow was going and so they began to worry, so they began leaving the key in the ignition outside the bar until one night they came out and the truck was gone, stolen, and right after that they threw in the towel on raising the car float which they never should have attempted in the first place, and the ice was out of the river by then so they got a tug to tow them back upstate."

"And they never heard nothing more about it," I said.

"That'd be right," Trevor said.

"Shit, I wonder what's the moral of that story?"

"Car floats can be a bitch, I guess," Trevor said.

***

It was well after dark by the time we got to Lock 17 at the tiny city of Little Falls. The city was once known for cheese processing and a hammer factory that closed long ago. Lock 17 is slightly more famous for having once had the highest lift of any in the world. It has since been surpassed by one in Kazakhstan, but it is still huge at 40 ½ feet. The city and the lock both owe their existence to a boulder strewn cataract of the Mohawk River which, even before the building of the canal, imposed a portage on all traffic up or down the river. A colonial town developed based around the waterpower derived from the falls and from the brief stoppage of goods detouring around it. By the late 19th century it was a flush little metropolis of cheeses and hammers, German eateries, and brawling canalers. But now it is much diminished, storefronts mostly closed, smokestacks cold and toppling.

Del woke me for my watch when we were about a quarter mile below Lock 17 and I made it up into the pilothouse just as we pushed into the long straightaway leading into the lock. A highway bridge crosses the canal just below the lock and for some reason the highway engineers placed a bridge column right in the right outer margin of the canal channel, right where the river forks off to the right and where there is always a sizeable eddy to complicate the task of maneuvering safely into the lock. All of our attention was focused on getting past the bridge column so that when we could once more look ahead to the entrance of the lock it was right upon us. This lock is unique in the canal for having an entirely different type of gate. While all the others have double leaved gates which swing open and shut horizontally, this one is built with a single massive portcullis, suspended in a framework towering above the lock. Approaching the lock, this massive gate blocks out all evidence that the lock chamber is open to the sky and, so, the effect on entering is that of venturing into a vast tomb. At night, under glaring floodlight, with cold water sheeting off the just raised portcullis onto the tug as it ventures in, the effect is magnified. The dreadful rumble of the gate as it descends is just the icing on the cake. There is no way not to think of doom.

Del and I handled lines out on the barge as we rose and rose up through the lock. Finally we floated level with the upper section. We spoke to the lock tender for a moment. He told us that we were the only traffic moving anywhere on the canal tonight. We told him of our intention to keep moving all night, and he said that he would call ahead to the locks farther down the line to be sure there would be someone on duty.

As soon as we were underway again, Del and Trevor went below to sleep while I took over steering. Alone in the pilothouse again, I threaded my way through the passage just above Lock 17 where the canal is carved into the rocky side of the gorge down which the river runs. In spots, the canal runs through a cluster of brick buildings on one side and ragged cliffs on the other. A mostly abandoned terminal lies dark on the left hand while to the right it is possible to glimpse the night bound city of Little Falls deep in the valley below. The river is smaller now and more circuitous, while the route of the canal shifts more and more often out of the river bed itself to man-made "ditch" sections recognizable by their directness and constant width. I wake Del to handle lines when we pass through locks 18 and 19 and, finally, around 4 a.m. we reach Utica. There, we pass through Lock 20 and enter the Rome level, 18 miles long and the highest altitude that we will attain on this trip, for now we have left the Mohawk River drainage and have entered the system of rivers and streams that flow into Lake Ontario, the St. Lawrence River and finally to the sea. All the rest of the locks will step gradually downhill for the 73 miles to Syracuse. The night remains surprisingly warm for November and there is no sign of the dense fog that often closes down the canal at this hour. The lock keeper at Utica tells me that as far as he is able to learn, the long passage down past Rome is clear and so I decide to continue on knowing that there is a reasonable chance that we will get into fog somewhere down the line. But up here on the Rome level, in the long man-made ditch where there is no current, no tide and the canal banks are evenly sloped, it is possible to hold up almost anywhere if the fog sets in so thick that it is impossible to go on. It is only necessary to nose the bow of the barge into the bank and have the deckhand run a line around a tree trunk or an overhanging branch. Once tied up it is possible to simply leave some lights on deck and go to bed.

The run down the Rome level is pretty simple. It is dead straight most of the way and the banks are uniform.

The deep loaded barge, as it pushes down the channel, piles the water up ahead of itself like a bulldozer, and the water then diverts down each side of the barge; rushing through the space between the steep canal bank and the side of the barge. The trick in steering is to keep the barge in the middle of the channel so that the same amount of water flows back down each side. If the barge gets a little off to one side, the bulk of the back flow shifts to the side with the wider gap and this reduced flow on the narrower side will pull the barge even farther to that side until the suction of the propeller pulls the stern of the tug up against the bank. Once the tug starts getting pulled sharply into one side or the other, the only way to correct is to quickly cut back the throttle to remove the suction. But there is a point of balance where the tug and tow are riding cleanly down the middle of the canal prism, the pressures are nicely balanced on each side and only the finest adjustments of the helm are required. It is entirely a matter of being able to feel when everything is in poise; and there is a pleasure in that.

The night is still, warm, and misty. With the two searchlights directed ahead – one trained on each canal bank – about 200 yards ahead, the voyage is condensed into a cone of light. The two searchlight beams reflect off of the mist to form a milky cloud of light and reflect off of the water surface ahead to create a wavering, almost hallucinatory projection on the passing forest. The pale green eyes of a deer shine from the brush, then the white flag of its tail flashes as it bolts. An owl launches itself from a high limb and crosses the water in a soft glide; and from both the banks, herons startle in the glare and fly off ahead, re-land and then startle again until there are a dozen flying in front of us at the outer periphery of the illumination.

The night wears on in this way until in the first of daylight we pass through the outskirts of the tired old city of Rome where a sprinkling of abandoned terminals and slips describe how the canal had once brought prosperity and business. The only sign of activity now is the big motor barge, DAY PECKINPAUGH, tied up along the bulkhead, deck lights on and exhaust streaming from its generators and pump engines. It is an odd looking vessel, built to transport liquid chemicals from Ontario, Canada into the canal, and so designed both to pass under the low bridges of the canal and to brave the often violent storms of Lake Ontario. It more resembles a submarine than a ship. Its pilothouse is mounted right up at the bow and to protect it from the weather on the lake it is everywhere equipped with heavy watertight doors and small round portholes set with inch-thick glass. There had once been many of these queer vessels working the canal and venturing out onto the Lakes and far down the Atlantic coast, but, now, the PECKINPAUGH, is the last survivor. A crewman is out on deck tending the pumps as the barge unloads in the first dawn light. He moves over to the rail as we drew near, one foot up on the bottom rung, and waves as we pass. Daylight is just coming up. It is still clear overhead but there is a bank of cloud spread across the western sky ahead of us. Trevor and Del are stirring in the forecastle below, the smell of brewing coffee drifting up through the hatch. My watch is done. Trevor comes up to take over steering.

"Made it to Rome, good going," he said. "420 feet in the air and now it's all downhill from here to Syracuse!"

"I hope," I said and went aft to check through the engine room. In half an hour I am asleep in my bunk below.

***

Way back, when I was serving my time as a deckhand, I worked on an old harbor tug that was owned by one of the few remaining independent tugboat operators in New York. The tug was a pre-war boat with the typical long deckhouse with the pilothouse set atop it. Down the

123

length of the deckhouse were a series of doors opening out onto the main deck. Forward on port and starboard sides of the deckhouse were doors leading into the galley, behind these, on both sides were doors leading into the upper level of the engine room; behind that on the port side, a door leading into the washroom and toilet and on the starboard side a storage locker. Behind this there were doors on each side which let into the cabins designed for the engineer on the starboard side and the assistant engineer on the port side. Each of these cabins, in addition to the door leading out onto the deck had a second door which opened into the upper level of the engine room so that the engineers could get quickly to their duty stations without having to go out on deck. Behind these two doors were those that opened into the deck hands' cabins – one on each side at the very back end of the house. These two rear cabins had only one way in and out and that was directly onto the main deck. This boat had been designed to work with a union crew of nine – Captain, mate, engineer, assistant engineer, cook, and four deck hands. Now, under more frugal times and non-union ownership, we were operating with a total crew of three. The owner, who served as captain and engineer, the mate who also served as assistant engineer and deckhand, and myself who served as deckhand, part time helmsman, and cook.

On this trip we had run light out of the harbor, down to Philadelphia to pick up two dilapidated sand barges which were to be brought back to New York to be scrapped. This was the kind of work that no one much wanted. It was the middle of winter and the two barges were in such bad shape that nowadays it would require special Coast Guard permits to move them anywhere. Nevertheless, at around 2 a.m. we arrived in Philadelphia after an uneventful 26 hour run from New York and in the early morning darkness located the two barges moored side by side on the Camden waterfront. Each of them was part flooded with water that had leaked into them either from the sea or from months of rainwater dribbling through holes in their decks. We tied up alongside and immediately set to work pumping them out, each of us taking turns tending the pumps while the others caught a few hours of sleep. By around daylight the barges were clear of water and an inspection by flashlight in each of the rusted dank compartments of the barges revealed that almost all of the leakage had come through the decks rather than through the hulls themselves. So, we packed up the pumps and began to set up the towing gear that we would need to get the scows back to New York.

Each barge was 120 feet long by 42 feet wide and without any cargo floated high in the water with only about two feet of draft compared to eight feet of freeboard. These barges were built identically at each end so that there was no bow or stern per se, but years of hard usage and damages had injured their integrity unequally so that one end of each was a little more seaworthy than the other, so someone had spray painted on the ends of each barge an orange "B" for bow or "S" for stern to warn who ever towed them which was most fit to take the greater punishment of serving as the bow. We shifted the barges around so that the one that appeared to be in the best condition would be the lead barge to be towed at the end of our 1200 foot main hawser. From the stern of the lead barge, a second 400 foot hawser would bring along the other barge. We set out all of this gear so that when we got underway it all would run out without tangling. Then we set out lights on the two barges, red and green on the bows of each and white on each stern.

By 9 a.m. we were ready to go. We had the outgoing tide and made good progress through the day down the Delaware River and Bay so that we were off Cape May by the time it got dark and then we swung our course north up the Jersey shore, 120 miles or about 15 hours to New York at our towing speed of about eight knots.

During the late afternoon as we approached the turn out of the Bay and into the winter Atlantic, the mate and I had gone around the deck of the tug and carefully stuffed rags into the various rust holes that perforated the lowest margin of the deckhouse where it joined the deck. This was a standard precaution that we took when venturing out of protected waters.

Whenever we went outside the harbor in that boat there was a certain degree of anxiety felt by the crew. It was an old boat and poorly maintained – the best that the captain could afford and maintained to the limit of what one man could accomplish on a schedule and budget skewed heavily in favor of alcohol. Nothing was repaired until it had failed at least once, and most repairs were, like the rags we pushed into the holes along the deck that winter afternoon, only stopgaps. The captain/owner viewed a tugboat like he would a hammer – you used it until you wore it out and then you went out and found another.

The mythical bond between the seafarer and his ship simply did not exist for my captain and for this, at sea, he was a very lonely man. He had once had a wife but she had gone. He had two daughters who avoided him. He had the friendship of his engineer with whom he drank beer with the same rote precision as the Mayans processed the hearts of their captives. The two of them had bought bright orange survival suits guaranteed to keep you alive forever in the coldest water. The captain had placed a pint of whiskey in the pocket of each, then he and the mate had hidden them someplace on the tug. Whenever the weather got particularly bad he would rattle my cage by asking where I had hidden mine, knowing perfectly well that I didn't have one.

So, I was off watch in my little cabin far back toward the stern of the tug as we made our way up the Jersey shore. I was to take over steering at midnight but lay unable to sleep because the wind had risen and the tug had begun to buck and heave in the steadily increasing chop. The chains that secured the heavy tire fenders along the side began to gnaw violently at the hull and with increasing regularity the bow would rise to a wave, hang dizzily, then with a twisting roll descend with a noiseless hush and bury itself in the oncoming chop. I could hear the waves slopping over the bow then sweeping down the deck just outside my door, pooling and hammering back and forth across the wide stern deck until finally draining back overside.

As the night went on the sea got worse, increasing from "choppy" to "sloppy" which are gradations of discomfort well below "rough" and in normal circumstances not considered dangerous, but this boat and this crew were not entirely normal and I in my lonely little cabin began to long for human company. The only way in or out of my cabin was the typical arrangement for a harbor tug of this vintage: a double "dutch" door which could be opened at the top to allow for light and ventilation while defending against any spray or slop coming in through the lower half. To make these doors weather tight there were thick rubber gaskets, heavy duty hinges and a massive lockset. But the panels of the doors were all warped and the rubber gaskets had long ago disintegrated into hard black pebbles. The doors leaked and, as the sea condition worsened, more and more of the cold Atlantic began to slosh into my cabin. Before long there were several inches of seawater playing back and forth across my floor and whenever the tug would take a particularly deep roll and ship a larger sea, the keyhole in the door would squirt an icy jet onto my bunk. It was still an hour before my watch began but I figured that if it got any rougher, I might not be

129

able to get out of my cabin at all; and certainly it would be more comfortable up in the pilothouse. I turned on the light at the head of my bunk, put on my clothes and gingerly opened the upper half of the outside door to estimate my chances of escape.

They were poor.

Every few seconds a wave would sweep aboard and flood the deck thigh deep and though it might be possible to drag myself forward along the side of the deckhouse using the handrail there I guessed that the captain or mate had probably sealed all of the forward doors from the inside and so I would be unable to get off the deck even if I were able to get forward. Instead, I figured that the best alternative was to climb out the upper half of my door, scramble up to the roof of the deckhouse and get to the pilothouse that way. I opened the upper half of the door, and reached up to grasp the two inch rim along the deckhouse edge. Then I hauled myself up to catch the lower and then the upper rungs of the railing above and in no time I was over the rail and safe from the welter below. Without my body to hold the cabin door open the next surge of wave and wind swung it shut and latched it with a crash. Clinging to the railing I made my way forward on the upper deck and let myself in at the door at the back of the pilothouse. The captain was in the helmsman's seat nursing a beer and the engineer lounging on the settee behind.

"We were just saying how maybe we gonna have to put on our suits and go back and get you so you could stand your watch, but here you are," the captain said; and both he and the engineer chuckled. "We were wondering if you were going to make it for your watch."

***

We were just past Utica when I awoke to the sound of the engine dropping to half throttle, rain pouring down onto the deck, and a sudden wind rattling things around. Del was sitting at the forecastle table eating fish stew while studying his newspaper.

"What's going on out there?" I asked.

"Wind and rain," he said without turning around.

"Where are we?"

"Just past Lock 21," said Del.

"Know why we're slowed down?" I asked.

"Trevor says he can't see anything." Del continued to study his paper as I got dressed and went up to see what was going on.

And there was wind and rain. A torrent, as if a fire hose was turned on us, engulfed the windshield. Trevor stood close to the glass and as tall as possible to see out at the very top where the glass was protected somewhat by the overhang of the wheelhouse visor outside. The banks of the canal were barely visible on either side and it was obvious why we had throttled back.

"Sorry to slow her down but there was a while back there when I couldn't see a thing," Trevor said while reaching over to boost the throttle slightly higher. "I think the weather has changed."

Within the hour the rain had eased to a steady drizzle and the wind disappeared but as the morning went on the temperature continued to fall sharply. A blanket of heavy featureless cloud hung over us and with a slow building certainty the west wind began to stir. Not far ahead the canal traversed the breadth of Lake Oneida, 16 miles of open water; all of it exposed to the west.

"This wind gets up much, we're going to have trouble with the lake," I said to Trevor.

"Just thinking the same thing," he replied. "You can see just that with the rain we had put enough water down in the barge to get it out of trim. Get ourselves out there on the lake with a whole bunch of spray, that thing will fill up like a bathtub."

"We can put a pump on it but I'm not sure it's a good plan to depend on one little old pump, if there's any kind of weather, to get us across."

"I don't think I'd trust ten pumps," said Trevor.

"Wait and see, I guess."

"Wait and see."

At Lock 22, the last before Lake Oneida, the lock tender took one look at our open barge and also warned us. "It may not look like much to you salt water guys," he said, "but it can still fool you." He also let us know that the motor barge we had passed that morning at Rome, the DAY PECKINPAUGH, had got underway and would be coming up behind us before long. The canal is a sleepy place and any commercial traffic moving anywhere is the subject of steady telephone gossip between the lock tending crews all up and down. When you enter the system at Troy it's not unusual to have the lock tender there inform you of a tow that has just entered all the way down at the other end at Tonawanda, 342 miles to the west on Lake Erie. He might then try to speculate as to exactly where, days from now, you would meet, and warn you to keep a careful lookout. To be informed of a vessel on the move only an hour or two behind is, by the standards of life on the canal, a veritable traffic jam. She would overtake us at the little resort town of Sylvan Beach at the entrance to Lake Oneida.

Entering the town, the canal adopts the course of what was once a marshy creek. It crosses a flat expanse at the edge of the lake and there is a long bulkhead with a paved margin to afford tie up space for vessels setting out or coming in from across the lake. Most of the way down this bulkhead is a low bridge crossing the canal and the margin and beyond this the canal lets out onto the lake, running for the first couple of hundred yards behind a stone breakwater. The wind was now blowing at gale force on the lake and a wall of spray swept over this barrier, blew across the channel and off into the low forest beyond.

Just as we were looking out at this scene the PECKINPAUGH came up behind us. She slowed down to pass us and as she crept by two crewmen were busy on deck stowing lines and securing hatches and doors. One of them waved to us and then made the gesture of holding in his breath and pinching shut his nose as he stepped inside the barge house and slammed the door behind himself.

"Looks like they're getting ready to go into submarine mode," Trevor laughed as the big motor barge forged out the channel. When it made the turn around the far end of the breakwater, exposing itself to the full effect of the wind, it disappeared into an overwhelming cloud of froth and spray. As it motored out of sight across the lake it looked like an ancient sea creature running half submerged, enveloped in a furious cloud.

"Don't make me go out there, Cap," Trevor drawled.

"I won't if you don't," I agreed. "I guess we'd better tie this thing up."

To get out of the wind we put out lines on the stretch of bulkhead behind the highway bridge and its embankment. As we did so I noticed that there was a young woman sitting under the bridge, her back to the abutment, wrapped in a bright yellow blanket with pink and blue teddy bears printed on it. Lying next to her was a big brown dog.

Once we were tied up and the engine shut down, we got out the gas pump and set it up on the barge to remove the rainwater that had collected down inside the cargo box. Once the water was out we left the pump in place against the time when we would set out across the lake. Then we all climbed ashore and walked into town to find some lunch and a phone so that I could call ahead to Syracuse to tell the customer that we were held up by the weather. We walked down the bulkhead margin, then climbed the embankment up to the highway to get to town and as we passed the bridge we got a better look at the girl huddled there. The dog raised its head and stared at us as we passed, while the girl gazed blankly at the water in front of her rocking slightly.

"What ya think?" asked Trevor.

"I'm guessing its one too many Grateful Dead concerts," I said.

The wind was blowing fiercely straight across the lake, over the narrow sand beach that formed the lakeshore, then across the road that we were on and right through the little town. Blobs of frantic brown foam churned up by the surf all mixed with sand, leaves and scraps of trash skittered across the road and the shallow waters of the lake – no more than 35 feet at any point down its entire length, were roiling to a muddy chocolate soup lathered everywhere with whitecaps and clouds of spray.

"It's like a miniature Lake Erie, the way the wind just tears it up," Trevor said. "You wouldn't think anything so small could look so bad."

Just a little ways down the road, just where the town was beginning to fill in on both sides of the street, we found a little restaurant that was open. The sign claimed that it was Italian, but it looked to be not much more than a pizza parlor; but that was perfectly good enough for us after eating our own cooking for a few days. Also, there was a decal on the window to indicate that there was a pay phone available inside. We went in and found all of the six tables empty and two girls standing around hoping for a customer. The building rattled and creaked in the wind. The seams around the door whistled like a Pan pipe.

"If you're here for lunch you can sit anywhere," one called.

"Anywhere you like," agreed the other.

We went to a table by the window that looked out across the empty street and the troubled lake. We agreed to share a large pizza, half mushroom and sausage and half anchovy. Trevor did the ordering and in the process began to lay on an unexpected helping of charm. First, he complimented her on the very welcome existence of her restaurant, and next on her youthful and pretty appearance.

She looked to be not much out of high school, not particularly pretty but willing to be friendly if for no other reason than to fill the boredom of a slow afternoon.

"Tell, me," said Trevor, "do you do that thing of kneading the pizza dough and then whirling it up in the air? If you do, I want to watch."

She giggled but replied, "No, I don't make the dough. The owner comes in early and makes up as many pies as he thinks we're going to need. If we run short, we call him, and he comes back and makes some more."

"I see," said Trevor. "And what does he do when he's not here?"

"He's the manager, and sometimes the bartender down at Ernie's. You know Ernie's? Down the street."

"I think I remember it. It's been a while since I was here. Anyway...." And Trevor gave her our order which seemed to go down fine until he got to the part about the anchovies. The girl's face scrunched up.

"Uh oh," said Trevor. "I'm thinking, 'No anchovies'."

She giggled again. "No it's not that, there's a great big can of them back there. It's just that if you want them you're going to have to put them on yourself 'cause Joy and I aren't touching them. They're disgusting!"

"I think we can do that, can't we, men?" Trevor was ecstatic. "Just show me to 'em."

Trevor, and the two girls went back into the kitchen to deal with the anchovies and I went to the back of the room to use the pay phone to call in to the customer in Syracuse and break the news that we weren't going to be delivering his cargo tomorrow. I took a moment to compose myself as these conversations could sometimes get ugly, particularly on these inland jobs where people were not so attuned to the kinds of weather-related delays that are far more common when working on the seacoast. All it takes is a good bit of wind from the wrong direction, however warm and sunny it may be, and no boat's going to go no matter how the customer might complain or threaten. Sometimes they swear up and down that they will find somebody else who will go in spite of the weather, but I've never actually seen that happen because if one operator is unwilling to go out, no other boat is likely to go to either. On top of that, there aren't very many tugboat guys who would take a job away from somebody else in a situation like that as it would just lead to a world where everybody would be forced to go out in weather that they knew they shouldn't.

But the minute I got the guy on the phone I sensed that this time it was different.

"I was hoping you'd call," he said. "Where are you? We've got a problem over here."

Hearing this, I also heard a squeal from one of the girls back in the kitchen, caused, I assumed, by inadvertent contact with one of Trevor's anchovies or else maybe he had thrown his head back and eaten one of them whole, like a frat boy swallowing a goldfish.

"We were setting up the crane this morning, getting ready for you tomorrow, and one of the laborers left a sledge hammer on the undercarriage. When the operator swung the crane around the hammer tore the oil pan off the engine, all the oil dumped out and the engine shit the bed. The crane's locked up and not moving until we rebuild the engine. There's a couple of guys down from Buffalo but it may be a couple of days before it's running again. So, I guess my question for you is, are you going to be able to wait around for them to finish up, and what's it going to cost me?"

A peal of laughter rippled through the restaurant. There was the hollow clatter of a large aluminum pot. What on earth is Trevor doing now, I thought while trying to concentrate on the question at the other end of the line?

Here I had called in to confess that I was going to have to hold up the schedule of the job because of weather, ready to absorb the loss involved in terms of my extra cost for food and wages only to find that the guy on the other side was in an even worse situation.

"Also," the voice on the other end of the line said, "I've got to get from you how you're going to want to place the barge so we can lift that thing off."

"I don't know," I replied. "I don't know the answer to either question at the moment. You see, we're right now on the east shore of Lake Oneida town of Sylvan Beach? And the wind's blowing like all get out and with this open barge we're not going to be able to get across the lake until at least tomorrow morning and maybe not 'til tomorrow evening. If it weren't for the wind we would have been to you right on time bright and early tomorrow morning, but now it's all a question of how soon we can get this barge across the lake without sinking it."

There was a pause as he absorbed this. "You're stuck," he concluded.

"Sounds like we're both stuck." I reminded him.

"Yup. And I guess we've just got to wait and see what it takes to get unstuck. You know, in the meantime I'd like to get together with you on how we're going to place this barge once you get it here. If you're just waiting around over there in Sylvan Beach I could take a run over there and bring you back here to take a look if that's all right. It's only maybe 40 minutes' drive."

I was, as always, staggered by the difference between tugboat time and real time.

"Yeah we could do that," I said.

"So, it's 1:30 now. How about I swing by at maybe 2:30. Where exactly are you?"

"We're tied up on the canal wall right where the highway crosses into town. I don't know the name of the road or the highway number but I think out here there's only the one of them."

"Got it. I'll see you in an hour," he said, and hung up.

I got back to the table by the window and Trevor was still not back from his adventure in the kitchen. Del was sitting there by himself and had taken the opportunity to get the Enquirer out of his pocket and resume his studies.

"Anything happening with that pizza?" I asked.

"Nope," Del replied without looking up.

But then Trevor reappeared. He sat himself down with a flourish. "We're all set," he declared. "First, we've got the pizza in the oven, which was no small accomplishment. Second, I found out what's what with this little town this time of year; and it ain't what it used to be but it'll have to do – so long as you like country music."

"Hank Williams," said Del.

"Around here, more like Garth Brooks," said Trevor, "but that's not the point; you see, all the young kids like those two out there are into rock and roll, Ozzie Osborne, or whatever, but Joy tells me there's Ernie's right down the street where there's country western, which is more our kinda crowd. We should check it out."

"Unless the wind drops out tonight, then we go tugboating," I cautioned.

"Oh, absolutely," said Trevor. "I want to get to Syracuse as much as you do, but I bet you anything that wind isn't dropping off for another 24 hours."

I didn't say anything about the crane being broken down, but I did tell them that I was getting a ride over to look at the site. The pizza came and we gobbled it down. It tasted wonderful. The girls were proud that they had braved out the anchovy challenge. They insisted on refilling our Cokes.

Once we were done, I got up to walk back to the boat, to make sure everything was OK there and to wait for my ride. Trevor and Del said they would take care of the check and then were going up the street to "locate" Ernie's country western saloon.

"Don't get in trouble," I advised. "And keep an eye on the boat."

Outside the wind was a whole lot stronger and colder than before. A scattering of clouds raced across the lake and every shadow that crossed the sun seemed to drop the temperature another point. The sour smell of fresh water spray was everywhere in the town. I got down to the embankment and walked along the canal toward the boat. I passed under the highway bridge where the young woman and the dog still huddled. The dog raised its head and stared at me guardedly as I passed. The girl just remained hunched, wrapped in her bright quilt, motionless, inert.

Standing on the walkway next to the boat was a man who watched me approach. He had an official look to him, a windbreaker and black polished lace up shoes.

"Good afternoon," I said to him.

"Good afternoon. You headed 'across the lake?"

"We were; but it looks like we'll have to wait."

"I wouldn't rush it," he said. "It's going to blow more before it blows less. Maybe snow."

"You think?"

"Seen it before." He reached into his jacket pocket and produced a badge. "Just wanted to stop by. You see that young girl down under there?"

"Yeah, what's her story?"

"Well I don't know exactly, but I'm sort of keeping an eye on her. She showed up here three days ago and hasn't moved. That dog took up with her since then, but I don't know what she's planning to do – maybe nothing; but I'm hoping that she'll pick herself up and get going again, 'cause if I get involved it'll mean taking her in, putting her in the hospital and god knows what all; and I'm hoping it doesn't come to that."

"I hear you."

He slipped the badge back into his pocket, "So I just thought I'd check in. Glad I caught you. I guess you're headed over to Syracuse with that thing?"

"Yah, in fact I'm expecting somebody from there to pick me up here in a few minutes."

"Well good to talk to you; take care, and remember, don't push your luck out on that lake. It has its fits, but always calms right down again."

"Thanks," I said to his back.

***

Over in Syracuse everything was at a standstill. As we drove through the gate of the canal terminal you could see the long boom of the crane slanting up into the sky. When we drove around the side of the shed we saw the rest of it, set up in the parking lot next to the mooring basin. It was a mobile crane, designed to drive on the road; "rubber mounted" as they say with tires rather than caterpillar treads. They had it all set out on its stabilizers and the boom up in the air when the engine had burnt up. Since the failure, in the same storm which had passed over us on the other side of the lake, the parking lot had been flooded and the crane now stood in the middle of a pool of rainwater which had in turn been befouled by all of the oil that had burst from the crankcase. Two guys in rubber boots were spreading straw on the water and raking it around to sop up the oil. Meanwhile the two mechanics had built themselves a little island of discarded wooden pallets underneath the chassis of the crane so that they could get at the engine without having to lie in the water. Their van was parked as close to the crane as possible. The rear doors were opened onto racks of tools and parts. On the floor of the van was an air mattress, a camp stove, and a cardboard box full of groceries. They already had the shattered oil pan removed

146

from the bottom of the engine and were probing around the crankshaft and rods to determine how much of the machine had seized.

Sean, my customer and chauffeur was tense. "Look at this fucking mess. Any of that oil gets into the basin and the DEC takes me away in handcuffs. And look at how the parking lot is sagged all around. We're going to be lifting 180 tons and what if this whole place collapses? This all used to be salt mines all through here and god only knows what's under there. We put the crane as close to the edge as we dared. Any closer and we're afraid the seawall will cave in, any farther back and the crane has to reach out too far. And now this; oil everywhere, and then a flood. How does it look to you?"

"You described it pretty well," I said.

There wasn't much else to say. I didn't want to tell him that, with the temperature dropping the way it was, pretty soon the pool around his crane was going to be a skating rink – with oil. As for the question of whether the crane would collapse into the canal basin or sink into the ground, I didn't know and it wasn't my job to know. I was just the tugboat guy. But I admit that I was curious; and certainly didn't want to get drawn into some kind of disaster that wasn't mine.

"Who told you that this was the place to set the crane?" I asked.

"The manager for this section of the canal. He told us this is the spot," Sean replied.

"Maybe this low spot means they lifted something heavy here before and if it didn't collapse then it won't collapse now. Is there anybody you could ask?"

"You don't know how tough it was to get all of this approved in the first place," Sean complained. "Now if I start asking questions the whole deal might fall apart. And if they come down here before I get this oil cleaned up they'll shut me down for good."

"Well, I guess when you get around to making the lift you should just pick up the weight of the piece but keep it placed on the deck of the barge and then wait a little and see if the ground holds. If it gives any you'll at least still have the barge under it. That's what I'd do, but it's not my call."

It was dark by the time Sean had me back to Sylvan Beach and the sky had glazed over with a low solid mass of cloud. The wind, if anything, had increased and hard little pellets of sleet rattled on the roof of the car and pebbled the surface of the road.

"Well, I'll give you a call in the morning and let you know how it looks for getting across the lake. It's all a question of when this wind drops out."

"Don't take any chances," Sean said as I got out of the car. "There's no telling when we'll be ready for you here, anyway."

"You neither," I said. "Good luck at your end."

***

The first thing I did as I walked down to the boat was to check to see whether the girl was still camped out under the bridge and I was relieved to see that although a lot of her stuff was still there, she and the dog were not. I could hear the tug's generator purring away and guessed that Del had started it to run the heating against the deepening cold. Through the pilothouse windows came the dim red glow of the light over the chart table, and the yellow deck lights gave the boat a warm beckoning appearance. I climbed aboard and found a note taped to the pilothouse door. In block letters that must have been Trevor's it said – DO NOT DISTURB! WE ARE UP THE STREET AT ERNIES. I looked in through the window and there on the pilothouse settee was the girl from under the bridge wrapped in her colorful quilt, asleep. Sitting bolt upright on the settee in the hollow behind her knees was the dog, watching me with alarm. I figured that if I stayed where I was the dog was going to start to raise hell so I climbed back down off the boat and headed into town to find Ernie's bar, which was not difficult because whenever you are looking for a bar in any small town upstate you just look for neon; and tonight, looking down the long beachfront road with the snow flying from left to right there was one small speck of a pinkish glow way down past the shuttered amusement park. During the ten minutes that it took me to walk there, I saw several cars pull in to the place and, in fact, that was pretty much the only traffic I saw moving on the street. When I got there, I found a big parking lot in front – mostly empty, and a big sign that said "snowmobile parking in rear". Just inside the front door there was a big entryway with coat pegs all up and down the walls and, above these, a stuffed fish which I guessed to be a Walleyed Pike. Past the entryway was a big low room with a long bar on the left, tables and chairs in the middle and a low stage and scrap of a dance floor on the right. The whole back wall of the place was glass sliders that let out onto a deck and, beyond that, the lake shore. The stage was empty but a twangy country western song was drifting off the sound system. Maybe it was just because of the cold ugly weather outside but the place had a soggy welcoming kind of feeling; full of cigarette smoke and beer in the carpet.

Trevor and Del were sitting at the bar way down by the back windows which I guess meant they could say they were keeping an eye on the weather. Del had his back to the room while Trevor had swiveled around to face out and was talking to a couple of ladies. He saw me at the same time I saw him. He waved, stood, nudged Del, touched one of the ladies on the shoulder to excuse himself and started across the room toward me.

"You saw my note!" he greeted me. "I didn't want you to be too surprised."

"Or bitten by the dog."

"Maybe that too. Let me tell you what's happening." And he sat down at an empty table in the middle of the room. Del also made his way over and sat down.

"You see," Trevor began, "after we finished our pizza and you left we had some left over so we packed it up and walked around a little, found this place, had a beer, and then went back down to the boat. That girl was still just sitting there under the bridge and as we were going by I stopped to offer her the left over pizza."

"Our leftover pizza," added Del.

"You had plenty," said Trevor. "And of course I was curious about what her story was, so even though she wasn't interested at first in eating or telling anything, Del went on back to the boat and I stayed and fed some of it to the dog and finally, some of it to her too."

"And then she told you her story."

"Some of it. Enough to figure the rest," Trevor said.

"And?"

"Well, seems she's here because she thought she had herself a boyfriend working here last summer. She ran away from home and came back here expecting him to be here from something he told her I guess; but he's not and so she's just kinda stuck under the bridge down there. Can't face going back home. No place else to go."

"Stuck in the pilothouse, right now," I pointed out.

"Well, yeah. I didn't know what else to do. She was cold, wet, hungry, and tired. You should have seen her. She was asleep the minute she put her head down."

"So what's the story with the dog?" I asked.

"Well, that's really just more of the same," said Trevor. "The same guy, the boyfriend, last summer he had the dog. When he snuck out of town he left the dog behind and when she came back looking for the boyfriend she found the dog instead, or I guess the dog found her, and he's been sticking with her ever since."

"Sounds like she's better off with the dog than with the boyfriend. She seemed a bit out of it when she was sitting under the bridge but I haven't met her yet."

"Oh you will," said Trevor. "'Cause I've put together a plan which I think you will like."

"I don't need a cook. I've got Del."

"No. No. Not that, though do you know that they used to do that all the time not so long ago. There were all these women and girls who would go on the boats and take care of things for the summer then get off in the fall without the companies back down in New York ever knowing anything. But that's not this. See, this girl's got a brother, older than her, lives right down the other end of the lake in Brewerton and we can hand her over to him as we're going through there tomorrow as soon as the weather eases up. So we can do a good deed and it's right on our way. What do you think?"

I could see that Trevor was really wrapped up in this thing, while Del, bless his heart was nodding along with the plan.

"You know, that all sounds nice, but this afternoon when I was down at the boat waiting for my ride to

Syracuse, the town cop was down there and kinda gave me the evil eye about her."

"What do you mean?"

"I mean he pretty much said that he's looking out for her and to stay away from her," I said.

"Well, then, why isn't she sleeping in the back of his patrol car rather than in our pilothouse?" Trevor was indignant. "Come on man, you got to do what you got to do."

"How old is she?" I asked.

"What does that matter? Nobody's touching her."

Del crossed his heart.

"Look at that," laughed Trevor, sealing the deal. "If anybody here needs a girlfriend, it's Del here and he's taken the pledge."

Several years before, I had a tow up to Seneca Lake. Up there the canal is little used and the banks are lined with trailers and shacks which once had been summer places but now more and more had folks living in them year round. It was a late autumn afternoon; sunny, crisp, and still; and as the tug passed one of these bungalow communities two young guys –early thirties maybe – emerged from a rickety screen porch and set out through the carpet of bright leaves blanketing their backyard. They walked toward the row of tall trees that bordered the canal. With them was a young black dog that scampered around their legs in excitement. One of the men carried a 22 rifle. Autumn is the time for squirrel hunting and I felt a glimmer of my own boyhood experience of going out on days like this hunting with my dog. But when they got down to the shore of the canal, one of them seized the dog by the neck while the other planted a shot through the top of its head. It shrieked and spasmed and they shot it again while it flailed on the ground. Then they slung it over the bank where it tangled in the brush at the water's edge; and they turned back through the dead leaves toward their shack.

"You know, it's hard to know how to tell a story like that," Trevor said. "I can see how you could laugh about it, but I guess it all depends on how you think about people in the first place."

Just then the lights over the little dance floor came on bright and the volume of the background music rose to take over the room. Apparently this was the signal that some in the room had been waiting for because one after another couples shuffled into the light to dance.

"Hey, this is getting lively," said Trevor. "You want to get something to eat here and see what develops?"

"Got to eat somewhere." I said. "I guess it's either this or more pizza."

Del got up to find a menu and Trevor went back to the bar to order more beer and to reconnect with the two ladies there.

An hour later we had finished our hamburgers, the two ladies had established themselves at a table across the room and Trevor was buying them drinks and taking turns dancing with them. It was some kind of Texas dancing which I knew nothing about but Trevor was good at it and both he and the two ladies were having lots of fun.

Pretty soon Trevor was back to us with the news that the ladies had suggested that we all go over to their place before it got too late. "I think they want to party a little more than this place allows," Trevor said. The music seemed louder, the lights brighter and the empty beer bottles littered our table. I knew right off that it was a stupid idea, but what was I going to do? Say no to somebody else's adventure? We paid up and headed for the door with the ladies leading the way.

But we were only maybe three steps into the parking lot when the situation completely changed. There was a police car right outside the door, engine running, and out of it climbed the cop who I had spoken to down at the boat that afternoon.

"I'd like to speak to you fellas a minute if I may," he said.

The ladies took one look at the situation and kept right on walking like they didn't know us, got in their car and were gone into the snowy darkness.

"I've decided to save myself the trouble of trying to figure out what you guys' intentions may be and I'm giving you the benefit of the doubt," he began. "I don't know if you all know it but that young woman down there has been going through some difficulty?"

"I was talking to her about that," said Trevor.

"I guess you did," said the cop. "So you may or may not know that she has a brother down the other end of the lake in Brewerton and I've been hoping that she would pick herself up eventually and go there."

"As a matter of fact, we were going to take her there as soon as the weather settles down," said Trevor.

"Well, that's very nice of you, but around here, nowadays, we use automobiles for that sort of thing; and seeing that the state trooper passes through here every evening, I got him to run her down there. Save you the trouble. I thought it was best."

"That was probably a good thing to do," I broke in. "We didn't think you were going to do anything like that."

"Oh no, we do what we have to do," he said.

"And what about the dog?" I asked.

"Oh, she took the dog with her. That's all to the good because the dog was getting to be a problem too; being stray."

"Two stones with one throw," said Del.

"What's that?" asked the cop, annoyed.

"Win, win," I said.

"Win, win," said he. "So, I hope you gentlemen enjoy your stay in Sylvan Beach. Please stay out of trouble and when you depart, be sure to look out for yourselves out on the lake. It can be tricky even though, as you know, we are far from the sea."

"Thank you, officer," said Trevor. "And thank you for helping out with that young lady. It was a good thing you did."

"Just part of my job, good night," he said, rolling up his window and driving slowly off.

'Well!" said Trevor as soon as he was gone. "And here I thought we were going to be the ones to save her. I think he may have misunderstood our motives."

"But then, he doesn't even really know us," I said, and felt a huge sense of relief that we had been simultaneously delivered of both the two ladies and of the girl. The dark cloud that had settled on our voyage had suddenly disappeared, leaving only the more straightforward challenge of getting the rest of the way to Syracuse. We set out down the street in the seething hiss of wind, surf, and sand. Del muttered something that sounded like "after the pleasure party", but I didn't really catch it. The red glow of the chart light still welcomed us. The note that Trevor had left for me was still taped to the pilothouse door, but below his message the girl had scribbled one of her own: simply, "Thanks".

***

It was another day before we were able to set out across the lake. During that time, it seemed that the momentum that had swept us along to Sylvan Beach had drained away. I got Del and Trevor to pursue small projects around the boat during the day, but nobody talked much. It's always this way, when you have to tie up for any length of time. The routine is broken, the sense of purpose is lost. It didn't help that all through that idle day the west wind boomed in from across the lake carrying with it squall after squall of heavy snow which pasted itself thick on every tree and building. The tug and barge were snowed in to a point where Del had to get out the snow shovel and go all around as if it were mid-winter.

"Lake effect" was what you heard from all of the locals. While racing toward us from the west the bitter wind that we were now enduring at Sylvan Beach had swept up huge quantities of moisture from Lake Ontario. This turned to snow, dumped savagely across the region. It was early in the year for this sort of thing, but not unheard of. The common wisdom claimed it meant an early freeze and a long winter. I wanted to get this job done and to escape back to the coast, to weather that I understood.

So, just after sundown of that second day, when, as is often the case, the wind let down, we got underway to cross Lake Oneida. Instead of pushing the barge across the lake as we had thus far, I decided tow it behind us, so that in the face of any chop the tug would be in front to break the way and to protect against water slopping into the barge. We would keep the towline very short so that the barge would be almost touching the stern of the tug and in this way we could keep a close eye on it and if necessary put someone aboard to run the pump.

We made our way out the channel. We passed through the lee afforded by the long entrance jetty and nosed out into the lake itself. The great wind of the two days before was gone and the water was glassy calm. We turned on the floodlight that bathed the tug's stern deck so that we could clearly see the barge behind us and it was obvious that there was no spray at all getting into it. It seemed that we had timed it just right and in a few hours would be safely across the lake with the rest of the night to cover the remaining distance to Syracuse. But even with everything seemingly in our favor, there is still − anytime you poke your head out beyond the harbor limit, and when in front there is nothing but dark − a feeling of dread. One captain I had worked under years before was routinely paralyzed by it during the lead up to a departure down the coast. While the crew would be getting the tug and tow ready to go, listening to the weather forecasts during the day to get an idea of what to expect, he would retreat to the bar and sit there, talking feverishly to whoever would listen, teller of sea tales, joker, weeper, all by turns through the day then, late, until closing. He would come back to the tug, sleep, then return to the bar at dawn. More than once the rest of the crew and I would entirely suspend our efforts, go home and wait to be recalled once our captain, like a knight on his way to the gallows, had reduced his fears to the salt of resolution. Once he had completed this sad alcoholic ablution, he would rally, call us out and the voyage would begin. But I do not believe that there is a seafarer anywhere who does not feel that ripple of terror when he is outbound and all of the welcoming lights are behind him.

"We got this one knocked, I think," Trevor remarked across the darkened pilothouse from his position at the helm. "Just 3 or 4 hours with the wind laid down like this and we've got it in the bag."

And an hour or so later, in the distance ahead, we could just begin to make out the lights of Brewerton at the far end of the lake. I went back onto the stern deck to check on the tow. The air was bitter cold and there was a skim of fresh ice on the deck. But the tow was riding along smoothly behind us, well protected. I went down through the engine room to check on everything and enjoyed the hot dry air that I found there with the bright overhead lights and the fine mechanical song of the engine. I checked gauges and laid my palm here and there to test its temperature. Passing through the watertight door from the engine room into the forecastle, I found Del sitting at the table reading a new copy of the *Enquirer* that he had obtained in Sylvan Beach.

There is a string of buoys laid out down the length of the lake, spaced about a mile apart, to mark the way across. At about half-way there is Shackleton Shoal well over to the left and then maybe five miles farther on there is a sprinkling of rocks called Pancake Shoal which even though it is well marked with lighted buoys still requires careful attention. Beyond this point the lake begins to narrow toward its outlet at the town of Brewerton and the range lights of the channel leading into the Oneida River become visible. At the speed that we were going with this tow it would be almost five hours to run the full length of the lake, Sylvan Beach to Brewerton.

Trevor steered down the lake keeping a good half mile distance to the right of the line of buoys. "You know," he said out of the darkness, "I hope I didn't overstep back there with letting that girl camp in here. I just couldn't see what else to do with the weather like it was and all."

"Well, it's just that I'd already had a visit from the town cop warning me to keep away from her; but you didn't know that. I tell you I was more worried about those two fine ladies in the honkytonk."

"My, didn't they melt away the minute they saw the cop. I'm guessing there was something more there than meets the eye."

"I think so too, and you know, I'm as much for having fun as the next guy but you've got to understand that I'm also trying to run a job here and the last thing I need is for you or Del or me to end up in front of the local judge."

"Yeah, I see that, and that's why I brought it up; so if I stepped out of line...."

"No don't worry about it. Nothing happened."

It's just, I wanted to do something to help her out. Who knows, she could have been my granddaughter."

"I thought of that, but don't worry. It all worked out."

"I hope so. You know, guys like us don't get the chance to do good deeds all that often. In fact it's so rare that I'm not even so sure I can tell when I do one."

"Well, chances are she wasn't yours anyway," I offered.

"Yeah, but she's somebody's granddaughter."

"I guess she is," I replied, and there the conversation petered out into silence until a little later Trevor reached over for the binoculars next to the steering stand and peered ahead for a long moment.

"You know," he said, "up until a few minutes ago I was seeing the lights down the far end of the lake, no problem; now I'm not. I'm thinking we've got another dose of snow coming. Snow, for sure, maybe wind."

"Oh brother, I hope you're wrong." He handed me the binoculars and it was obvious that the lights of Brewerton were gone though most of the line of buoys that we had been traveling along were still in sight. "Looks like it's time to do a little navigation," I said.

The book, showing the length of the canal, was lying on the chart table, open to the full page which showed the lake, its hazards and its buoys. I switched on the chart light and went to work establishing as accurately as possible our position as of that moment. The map bore much less information than a coastal chart, but in a couple of minutes I had our position marked out exactly and then consulted the log book to figure precisely what our speed had been since clearing the jetty back at Sylvan Beach. Then I had Trevor steer very carefully toward the farthest out buoy that we could still identify and wrote down the compass heading so that if the visibility suddenly was lost we would have a good heading to steer on and would know our forward speed: dead reckoning, as it is called.

"OK now, Trevor," I said once this was done. "I'd like you to get on a course of 274 degrees which should carry us right to the light on the gap across Pancake Shoal."

"274 it is, Cap," said Trevor with a new seriousness in his voice.

After we had gone another 15 minutes a fine snow began to sift through the glow of the tug's running lights and the west wind, so light just moments before, began to pick up. I got one last fix of our position from the buoys that remained last visible and then we were flying blind.

"Bet you wish we had that radar up on the roof right now," said Trevor.

"I was thinking of sending Del to set it back up, but he'd probably just electrocute himself; and, anyway, we're in good shape. I'm pretty good at this piloting stuff."

"Glad you are," said Trevor, "'cause not too many nowadays do it enough to keep good at it what with GPS and radar and all. It's been years since I did any."

"I do quite a bit of work outside of the harbor and up and down the coast so I'm still in the habit of thinking that way anyway, so we should be ok. And here at least on a lake you don't have any tide and current so that makes it easier."

"Well, you tell me the course you want and I'll steer it for you, by God. Don't worry about that."

"Very good," I replied, while out in front of us the surface of the water began to show here and there the first beginnings of little wind-streaked ripples. And the tug was beginning to come alive to the wind as well. The rigging began to hum quietly. The spinner head at the top of the stove pipe began to squeak; all of these gave subconscious notice that the wind was coming back to the lake. Up ahead, one small whitecap appeared at the thin edge of illumination thrown from the running lights. It jumped out of the darkness like a white imp, rushed past the bow and was gone astern. The snow flew ever thicker against the front window and Trevor switched on the wipers. Del emerged from the forecastle where he had been studying his newspaper. He had already put on his foul weather gear and a stocking cap.

"Hi Del," I said.

"What you got for me?" Del asked with a tone that suggested that he already knew perfectly well.

"We're going to need to keep an eye out for water getting into that barge. Probably need to pump it some."

Del nodded, "That's what I figured."

"We've got a full can of gas up there so you can run the pump pretty much all you want. Just make sure the water doesn't get ahead of you."

"Right, Cap." Del selected a flashlight from the shelf at the back of the pilothouse, testing one after another until he found one with fresh batteries and a strong beam. Then he and I went back to the stern deck. The cold and spray had grown little icicles hanging from the side rail of the tug, and the stern deck was slick. Trevor slowed the tug and then backed it down until the stern was pressed up against the barge. Del clambered onto the barge, as I stood ready to help him if necessary. Once he was safely across Trevor eased the tug ahead once more and gradually brought the throttle back to full ahead. A steady curtain of light spray whipped over the front of the barge and rattled off of the blue tarp covering the cargo. Del reported that there was about six inches of water collected down in the forward corner of the hold where the hose of the pump was positioned from the rainstorm two days before. He gave a couple of pulls on the starter cord and the pump sputtered to life. He drew up a bucket of water from the lake and poured it into the body of the pump and then stood back while the pump dealt with this priming charge, engine clattering wildly and the pump itself belching foam until it found suction. The pump engine sank into a steady determined beat and a solid two inch stream of water gushed from it back into the lake where it belonged. It took only about three minutes before the pump was sucking air, and Del shut it down, but within the space of those three minutes the wind had risen a little more and the size of the waves that beat against the barge increased. I was about to signal to Trevor to back the tug down against the barge once more, when Del called over that he might just as well remain up there as it wouldn't be long before the pump would have to be run again.

"You be careful up there," I shouted. "Shine your flashlight if you need us to do anything."

Del waved and climbed down the ladder into the hold of the barge to find shelter from the wind and the spray. For the next two hours while we struggled down the lake he would appear on deck from time to time to start the pump, each time pumping longer until after about an hour it ran constantly, throwing a solid stream of water over the side while at least as much sloshed back aboard.

We were in serious trouble. The wind slowly rose and the chop on the lake increased until there was a steady flood of spray striking the pilothouse. The snow continued thick and blowing so that visibility was reduced to zero.

There was a very real possibility that our barge with its big blue thing was going to end up at the bottom of the lake, a home to walleyes, crawdaddies, and eels. The only advantage we had was that the tug itself breasted away most of the force of the waves and thus protected the barge from the worst. And, slowly but surely, we were making progress toward shelter at the far end of the lake. The closer we crept toward that far shore, the less the chop and the better our situation. Even as the wind steadily increased, the sea conditions worsened not quite as rapidly. Twice during the two hours we struggled westward I had Trevor alter course a few degrees to the right to compensate for what I estimated to be the increasing effect of the wind blowing us off course. When we had run out the time I estimated that it would take us to reach the red flashing beacon that marks the passage through the shallows at Pancake Reef, I switched off the running lights to see if we could see its flash; sure enough, it was just visible through the driving snow just off to our right. I switched the lights back on, jotted down the time and had Trevor alter course to the left to take us to the entrance channel into Brewerton.

"You get a gold star for that one," Trevor said. "I was steering just as carefully as I could but I never thought we'd see that mark."

"Well, you steered good enough," I said. "Another hour of this and we're off the lake and out of trouble"

Although the snow and wind had not let up at all, the chop on the lake got steadily less as we made our way up into the narrow part of the lake. Del was no longer running the pump constantly. He was now most of the time out of sight, out of the weather down in the hold of the barge. I imagined him holed up under the blue tarp, somewhere deep inside the generator, reading his paper by flashlight.

It was 1 a.m. when we finally made it into Brewerton, dragging the barge behind us. In the wide part of the harbor we throttled back and maneuvered to get the barge off its towline and back to pushing again. When this was done Del climbed back aboard stiff with the cold and staggered down into the engine room to warm up.

"There's just a couple of miles down to Lock 23 and there probably won't be anybody there to lock us through this time of night so we'll tie up there and catch a nap, then polish off the last of the distance in the morning."

"Sounds good to me," said Trevor. "I'm just glad to be off that lake. Christ, what a place."

As we pushed past the wharf at Brewerton a parked car started up, flashed its lights twice and drove off.

It was just after 2 p.m. the next afternoon when we finally arrived at the Port of Syracuse. It was a weird semi-abandoned place which had once been a turmoil of oil, salt, and grain operations. Now pretty much desolate. All day the sleet and snow squalls had continued, and the entire countryside was covered with a concrete-like hardened slush. The sky was one heavy grey cloud, bleak and forlorn. Pushing down polluted old Lake Onondaga toward Syracuse at its southern end we passed the power plant in which our generator would eventually be installed. Dull grey steam trailed flat from its tall stacks in the harsh wind. But to get it there, up among the steaming concrete hulks clustered on the western shore of the lake, we first had to put it ashore at the only piece of solid ground available; the canal terminal down at the end of the lake. We barely squeezed under the railroad bridge that crossed the entrance to the terminal and as we did we also scraped along the silty bottom of the channel, so little used was the Port of Syracuse these days.

In the parking lot of the terminal the crane was still sitting in what had now become a broad frozen lake in which was entombed a litter of coffee cups, sandwich wrappers, pizza crusts, and cigarette butts. The mechanics were still hard at work finishing up the repairs. They had rigged a crude tent of plastic sheeting between the open back of their van and the crane and in there they had installed a kerosene blower that sent a jet of fume-laden heat throughout their primitive encampment.

"I didn't know where you'd gone," said Sean. "I called down to Sylvan Beach and they said you weren't there anymore and you weren't in Brewerton; then, finally, I called over to Lock 23 and they said they'd locked you through. So now you're here and we're just about ready; so maybe things are looking up."

"Glad to be here," I said.

"I didn't think you were going to be able to make it across the lake so soon."

"It laid down just after dark last night so we went. Snow came on again before we got across, but not too bad. Anyway, here we are."

The riggers climbed aboard the barge as soon as we had it secured to the terminal bulkhead. They set up their wire bridle and were ready to make the lift as soon as the crane was running again. They had a big hydraulic trailer – like they use for moving a house – to put the generator on. The crane engine started up while the two mechanics hovered around it checking gauges and inspecting for leaks, then started to load their tools back into the van. The crane operator climbed up into the cab and gingerly tested the controls, left and right, up and down, then, satisfied, swung the hook out over the barge and nodded to the rigging foreman. They shackled the lifting bridles into the hook and the operator began to take a strain. Slowly the barge rose up in the water as the weight of the generator ever so gradually transferred to dry land. The writing on the side of the barge reemerged until, finally, the generator was just free of the barge and hung by an inch over the timber stringers that had borne it in the hold. At this point the lift was halted and both Sean and the rigging foremen searched all around the crane for any sign that the pavement might be giving way. Everything was fine and they gave the signal to continue the lift. Once entirely free of the barge the crane operator boomed up and then swung the load over land to bring it in line with the trailer, then very slowly lowered it into place while the rigging crew slid timber blocks beneath it to take the weight. The entire lift took no more than ten minutes and except for shifting the now-empty barge to the back corner of the terminal our job was done.

I began to think about the return trip to New York. Trevor would be getting off here in Syracuse; catching a bus to New York to begin his regular two week shift on Wednesday. Del and I would spend the rest of this day getting Trevor to the bus, picking up some groceries, a new Enquirer, and getting some sleep before starting back down the canal early next morning.

At the bus station I paid Trevor in cash. He tucked the bills into his shirt pocket without counting them.

"It was a pleasure working with you," I said. "It made the trip a lot easier."

"Hey, it was a good trip, some ups and downs but it's always that way on the canal, isn't it? Good to get out here again, relive old memories and such."

"Yeah, I could see that."

Trevor turned to get on the bus, but turned one last time, "Oh and nice job getting us off the lake in one piece last night. That was quite a ride."

"Good steering," I said.

"That's the easy part. I hope we can do it again sometime."

"Me too."

"Have a safe trip back," and Trevor climbed up on the bus and was gone. At the time I expected that we would be able to work together again, but later that winter I heard that he was taking time off the boats. Throat cancer, they said. Not long after I heard he had died. I don't know if he knew about it during our trip together. I like to believe that he did.

Walking back alone from the station there was one spot from which I could get a view of the western shore of the lake. It was steep and clustered here and there with trees. Far up there, moving at a glacial pace with yellow warning lights blinking was a convoy of heavy vehicles at the center of which was the generator beneath its trim blue tarp, slouching like some prehistoric snail toward its final destination. After staring at that object for so many days and nights in so much different weather, right there in front of me, it startled me to see it far over there on the hillside, like a big runaway. It was not my responsibility any more, I understood; but it still felt that some part of it belonged to me.

***

Next morning at 4 a.m. we got underway. The wind had finally gone calm. The sky had cleared off and the temperature had dropped sharply. As the tug hurried through the bends of the Seneca and Oneida Rivers the heat of its stack set off the infra-red burglar alarms at cottages all up and down the shore. Porch lights snapped on and off and dogs barked in fierce contagion. In the future lurked cell phones, GPS, the trade towers; things would soon become abnormal but right then, just about dawn, passing once more through Brewerton, where the water had lain still all night in the cold, there was a brittle skim of ice. The stem of the tug chiseled through it as if it were fine virgin glass and scattered a bright tintinnabulation from shore to shore.

As we steamed through the sleeping town, just as the sun rose up on the far side of the glassy lake, on the second floor of a home that faced into the new golden light, a woman drew apart her thick blue velvet shades and stood for a moment radiantly naked; watching as we passed. But when I turned in the helmsman's chair to get a better look she must have seen me because with a flick of the curtain she was gone.

"An I for an I"

We got underway from Red Hook, Brooklyn with two scows alongside. Each was 160' long, 42' wide, and 8' sides. One of them had a crane set up on it plus an air compressor, a generator, a blue and yellow Port-a-san, and two 20-foot containers - one for tool storage and the other to serve as a hooch for the work crew once it got to the job site. The second scow had three big stacks of creosote treated timber plus a dozen black steel barrels of galvanized hardware – bolts, spikes, turnbuckles and tie rods. Everything on both barges was lashed down six ways to Sunday. My deckhand, Beth, and I went up and down the length of both scows, kicking the wire lashings to see that they were tight, then we cast off the dock lines one by one and walked them back from the edge of the deck and coiled them down on top of the machinery, on top of the hardware barrels, the catwalk of the crane; anywhere where they would be safe from being washed overboard. It wasn't necessary to take all of these precautions when towing around in the harbor, but this tow was headed out the East River and then out Long Island Sound to the Connecticut River, and that could be a different story.

We idled the tow out of Erie Basin with the crane barge alongside the tug's port side and the material scow out ahead then throttled up a little in Red Hook Channel, then once we made the sharp turn into Buttermilk Channel and the East River and the span of the Brooklyn Bridge lay before us, I finished throttling up. Straining hard against the three lines securing it to the scows, the tug rolled into the tow and the tug's propeller began to rumble in the turbulent flow of water passing under the barges. The flood current was just beginning to stir and swept us up the length of the East River with ever greater speed. It was mid-April, just before noon. I figured to be at our destination at about 7:30 the next morning, give or take a few minutes. We would be less than an hour securing the tow at the job site, then the run back of nine hours to be back tied up by 5 or 5:15 in the afternoon. About 29 hours all told.

"You think we'll be able to keep it alongside the whole way?" Beth asked so as to make her own plans as to what we were going to need to do.

"No, I think we're going to have to put it on the hawser. I don't want to have to get into a Chinese fire drill in the middle of the night," I said. "We'll tow it with the crane barge first, then the material scow set out behind so you might as well start setting it up while we're going out the river."

"Put lights on both of them?"

"Yeah, we'll need the lights on both and you better get those two heavy lines out so we can use those between the two scows. I don't want to trust their lines."

All the way out the East River there was a big oil company tug and barge pushing along about half a mile behind us with a helper tug shadowing it; the big tug had throttled back to be moving at the same speed as us so that there would be no need to arrange a passing while we made our way out through Hell Gate.

The forecast was pretty good for overnight, ten to 15 knots southwest, one to two foot sea. All day the sky had been clear but now in the late afternoon there was a wash of haze off to the south, way up high. It suggested that the actual amount of wind overnight might be on the high end of the forecast, and this was a cause for worry. It was a long way to the mouth of the Connecticut River, most of the way down the Sound where it was wide open to the weather. Because the shortest distance was straight down the Connecticut shore, we could expect the north side of the Sound to be increasingly exposed to the effects of any significant breeze from the South, and that was exactly what was forecast. Tonight, because we were obliged to tow down the exposed side we would need to be prepared for whatever conditions we might encounter.

If we had been towing just a single scow there would be no problem. The tug was equipped with a hydraulic winch that stored 1200 feet of wire rope, which was tremendously strong and, with the help of the winch, easy to handle. The lead barge, the one with the crane and the other machinery, would be towed on the wire and would be secure in any conditions that we might encounter on this night. The second scow, the one with the materials, however, required more care.

In the placid waters of the Harbor, two scows can be towed as a single unit, lashed close together one behind the other. In rougher conditions, however, these lashings have not the stretch and flexibility to withstand the wave action. It is necessary to separate the two scows by a distance that increases according to the roughness of the conditions. The sand and gravel companies which routinely operate on Long Island Sound will usually put out about 20 feet of very heavy, doubled rope between their scows. If conditions are expected to be worse than the security expected from this method, they simply postpone their trip. If a tug must take more than one barge in rougher weather, then it is necessary to rig a long hawser, reinforced with wire wherever there is a possibility of chafing on the bow and stern of the scows. To rig up such a system requires a lot of time and equipment. To recover it all at the end of the trip requires at least an equal amount of time and effort and so I wanted to get away without setting up this sort of gear for just an overnight trip down the Sound. But what would be good enough?

So, when we got to the open stretch between the Stepping Stones Light and Execution Rock it was time to switch from towing the scows alongside to towing them astern. Beth was standing by, leaning against the chart table.

"I guess we better get this thing on the wire," I said to her.

"Yep," she said and reached for her work gloves.

I slowly dropped the engine down to half throttle, waited for our speed and heading to settle down and then switched in the autopilot to hold our course while we got to work. I climbed up onto the barge while Beth went back to the stern deck. She passed the ends of the two towing bridles up to me and I dropped them over the corner bits of the lead barge. She had already brought the battery powered lights from their charger in the engine room; 2

red, 2 green, and two white; and had set them up in their proper positions on the barges. They had photo-cells which would switch them on as it got dark.

"You better hand up the ends of the two heavy lines coiled up there on the deck house while you're at it," I said.

"So this is going to get serious, eh?"

"I think, maybe," I said. "It's going to be pretty open down there where we're going."

"Here you go," she said, handing up the end of the first line.

Both lines were three inches in diameter. I had spliced a four foot eye in each of the four ends and had been very careful to make them identical in length at 120 feet each. They were far stronger than the lines we normally used for making up tows, though much more difficult to handle because of their diameter and weight. They were reserved for unusual occasions when you needed some worry medicine. I hung the eye of the first line over my shoulder and started down the length of the barge, drawing the line out behind me until I reached the far corner where the second scow was secured. I dropped the eye and walked back to grab another bight of the rope and drag it up to the corner also. Beth meanwhile was hauling the second line over to the other side of the seam between the scows.

"I guess we'll put out three parts," I called across to her. "40 feet between them should be plenty if it comes to that."

We removed all of the lines holding the two barges tight together except at one point which could be easily released when the time came, then we laid out the heavy lines between the corners of the two scows so that the lengths were divided evenly in thirds with the slack laid out on deck so that it would stream out properly. Then I went back onto the tug and slipped the engine into neutral and let our speed drop off until we were barely drifting ahead. Beth let go the single line holding the two scows together, then came back to help me cast off the lines holding us alongside the tow. Finished with this, she scrambled back aboard the tug and I steered the tug so that it sheared away from the scows as they continued to drift slowly ahead. Once the tug and the scows had separated and the only thing connecting them was the bridle and tow wire, which began to pay out on the stern deck of the tug, the heavy wire and towing shackle banged and sparked as it yanked across the deck and over the stern behind. I put the rudder hard over and nudged the throttle ahead for one short thrust to swing the boat around so that we came around to face directly away from the scows. The tow wire pulled taut, rolling the tug a few degrees while I nudged the engine ahead once more. The bridle and tow line remained taut. The scow with the crane – the lead scow now – ceased its drift and fell into line behind us. The material scow continued drifting, pulling out the three parts of line until they too came taut. We were now, momentarily, heading back in the direction we had come from.

"Geez, Cap, we're headed the wrong way," Beth joked.

"Damn, how'd that happen?" I laughed as I nudged the helm over to starboard and began a wide easy turn of 180 degrees that soon had us heading out the Sound with the tow stretched out behind us.

"How much wire do you want to put out?" Beth asked.

"Make it 600 feet for now," I replied.

She stepped out on deck and made her way aft to the winch. There, she switched on the hydraulic valve and released the brake. The wire pooled smoothly off the winch drum while the tug idled ahead. When she judged that 600 feet had run out she raised her arm and I took the tug out of gear. She put the winch brake back on and the small remaining forward momentum of the tug pulled the long catenary of the tow wire clear of the surface. It hung there for a second or two, almost straight and then began to lose tension and splashed back down to the surface once again. As it did I levered the engine once more slow ahead, catching the tension of the wire and holding it. Slowly I increased the throttle until we were full-out once more and with the tow stretched out far behind. The tow wire rode just under the sea surface for the middle third of its length and we rolled ahead at a speed of just over five and one-half knots.

As I always did whenever I passed Hart Island in daylight I took a minute to examine the shoreline with the binoculars. Right out at the southernmost tip of the island, standing upright among boulders, is the rusted bulk of an ancient diesel engine; all that remains of one of the many tugs owned by Captain Bill Davis, best remembered for having been owner of a total of 21 tugboats over a long career – all of which sank. This particular boat had been lost while towing a dredge one winter night. Bill had struggled along as it came on to snow and the sea worsened until finally the thrashing that the tug was taking loosened a fuel fitting and the engine died. Adrift with no possibility of getting the engine restarted, Bill had figured that any obligation he had had with the dredge was void and he cut it loose to seek its own fortune along the rocky Connecticut shore while he, in the tug, would accept their own fate independently. As it happened, the dredge washed ashore on the finely graded sands of Orchard Beach and suffered not a scratch while Bill's boat fetched up on the stones of Hart Island and became a total wreck. Bill and his dog Bruno were able to wade ashore and make their way through the storm to the house of the watchman assigned to Potters Field, New York City's cemetery for the indigent, unknown, and unclaimed. The poor lonely man is said to have fainted in superstitious terror when Bill hammered at his door in the wee hours. Now, decades later, only the husk of the engine remains.

Captain Bill took it all in stride. He went on to sink many more tugs by one mishap or another. Staunchly independent, he ended his days living on a dilapidated cabin cruiser in a Jersey City backwater.

"There's that old engine again," Beth chided me as I put the binoculars back in their box mounted on the side of the steering stand.

"Just keeping myself honest," I replied. "By the way, who's taking care of the cat?"

"My boyfriend's got her this time," Beth replied. "Problem is he's also got his damned snake, like the kind that eats little kids in Borneo. I never know if I'll have a cat when I get back. Or just a bigger snake."

Though I had never met the boyfriend, I did have a relationship of sorts with the cat. Twice, when Beth had not been able to find anyone to care for it when she and I had been called off on longer jobs, she had brought the thing aboard in its carrier. What with the engine noise and the constant motion it had never been able to get comfortable on the boat and whenever it was let out of its box it would prowl relentlessly around the pilothouse, yowling and unhappy. We were afraid that if she got out on deck she might leap over the side or else disappear into the engine room and never come out.

"You know, if you're stuck you can bring her along any time. If she can stand it, I can."

Beth was easily the best deckhand I had ever had. She was absolutely reliable; showed up at the boat whatever our starting time, night or day. She kept her eyes open, learned quickly, never complained, and talked little. She lived someplace in Brooklyn and traveled to and from the boat by gypsy cab. She'd grown up someplace around Boston, had worked on several windjammers, crossed a couple of oceans. On the nape of her neck she had the tattoo of a cat, sitting tight with an empty thought balloon above its head. That's about all I knew about her.

***

By the time the sun set we were nearly as far as Bridgeport. The haze that had been barely noticeable back when we had put the tow on the hawser had now overspread the sky so that the sun had already lost its authority well before it dipped below the horizon behind us. The wind remained light from the southwest and the sea was only rippled, though grey and cold. Beth had steered for a couple of hours while I went through the engine room, checking through everything to make sure that we were ready to run through the night. After getting through in the engine room I moved forward, through the watertight door into the forecastle to prepare something to eat. I'd bought a rotisserie chicken and a half a pound of potato salad from the store the night before. I spun the chicken in the microwave to warm it up, then slapped together a couple of plates and brought it up to the pilothouse along with a couple of cans of Coke.

"I'll steer if you want to eat," I said.

"It's just running on autopilot anyway. I can stay here," Beth said.

I passed her the plate and sat down on the settee behind her with mine in my lap.

"We're making pretty good time at the moment," I said, "and I guess we'll pick up the ebb current pretty soon."

"It seems like we've got plenty of time to get there."

"Oh yeah, we don't want to go into the river until low water slack so sometime after midnight we'll be able to throttle back, but for now we'll keep it hooked up and get a ways farther along."

The light was draining out of the sky and the shore lights began to appear. Stratford Point, Middle Ground, and Old Field Point far across the Sound all were just becoming visible. Looking astern through the back windows of the pilothouse, the lights on the tow were discernible now, two reds, two greens and now and then when the scows swung a little in the tug's long wake, a glimpse of one of the two white stern lights. Up on the mast of the tug burned the three white towing lights announcing our presence in the rising night. Far out in the middle of the Sound the big tug and barge that had followed us out the East River earlier in the day had now put its barge out behind on a quarter mile of wire. After slowly ramping up its throttle it had now passed out ahead of us bound for the Cape Cod Canal and on to Portland, Maine. As it came to full throttle its exhaust had darkened with soot until now it cast a grey slick into the wind that spread downwind in a distinct thin layer which undulated with the currents of the atmosphere, just as the surface of an uneasy sea forms a long meditative swell. With calligraphic solemnity the big tug's smoke revealed, like a droplet of dye in a flowing spring, the working of the wind.

After we had finished our dinner I took over steering while Beth stepped outside with a bucket of fresh water, a rag, and a squeegee to clean the salt film off the pilothouse windows.

"Thanks for doing that," I said. "This night's developing a funny look."

"It's gotten chilly out there, and there's a lot of sparkle in the lights off to the east," Beth observed; and it was true. The lights on the far off tug and on the distant shore all had that intense quivering look that foretells an unsettled night.

"If you don't need me for anything, I think I'm going to get some sleep," she said.

"Thanks. You go ahead and I'll give you a call around midnight."

"Just give me a shout," she replied and went below.

Alone now, I spent the next while tidying up the chart table at the back of the pilothouse setting out the charts that would carry us through the night; the large scale plan of the eastern half of Long island Sound which began just about four miles ahead of where we were at that moment, the smaller scale chart of the area around the mouth of the Connecticut River, and then the chart of the lower reaches of the river itself. I laid them out one on top of the other in the order that I would need them; then I gathered the piloting tools from the chart drawer – parallel ruler, dividers, and a pencil – and set them out on the ledge at the back of the table.

Finished with that, I adjusted the light levels of the engine gauges, the radar screen, and all the other instruments dimming them until they barely glowed in the gathering darkness. Then I settled into the helmsman's chair and scanned out ahead into the dark. The glare of the ruined town of Bridgeport was now just behind. The tall stacks of the power plant there streamed a ribbon of pale smoke, almost flat, suggesting a stronger wind aloft than what we were feeling right now on the water. Ahead were the beacon lights of Stratford Point on the left and Middle Ground on the right. An unlighted bell buoy lay someplace right ahead and I scanned the path ahead with the binoculars until I was able to pick out its dark shadow just to the left of our course – just where it was supposed to be. We were settled down on course to carry us straight on down to a point a mile outside of Faulkner's Island then on to a point one mile to the left of the buoy marking the west end of Long Sand Shoal. From there it was another six miles to the Connecticut River mouth and the first hints of daylight would be low in the sky right ahead.

***

Just behind the boulder strewn bluff and confident lighthouse of Stratford Point, in the fold of a broad shallow bay, was the mouth of the Housatonic River. I knew well how the buoys along the edges of its channel wagged and veered in the suck of the current. Through the years of working all over this part of the coast I had grown familiar with the approaches and leads of most of its rivers. I could recite the sequence of buoys in each, the steering marks, and the scatter of obstructions. It was all part of the knowledge required by the trade. But there are some places

194

that have struck a deeper mark than others, verging on horrid intimacy; this obscure inlet was one of those.

Years before, when I had owned my little wooden tug, I had spent a long cold winter on a bridge repair job up there. My boat had been hired to tend the floating equipment on the job site which consisted of only a small barge with a crane mounted on it and an even smaller material scow. For my little boat these two barges seemed plenty big enough at the time. There was a crew of six guys, more or less, depending on what stage of the job we were at; and our task was to rebuild the timber fender work in the opening span of the railroad bridge that crossed the river at Stratford. There was a disused sand and gravel yard a quarter mile upstream from the bridge which we used for a staging area for the job and it was there that the men would assemble every morning at 7:30. I would meet them there and ferry them down to the bridge.

Though most of the time the two barges were tied up to the bridge fender, working on the repairs, I would frequently be called upon to tow them up to the staging area to put something on board or to take it off. And besides moving the barges around, I would shuttle the work crew to and from the job site. Then during each day there were occasional shifts required so that the crane and material barges were best located on the job. But more important than this routine shifting was the occasional necessity of removing the two barges from the opening channel of the bridge to clear the way for any vessel traffic moving up or down the river. The repair job had been scheduled for winter rather than summer so that there would not be a steady stream of pleasure boats to disrupt our work, but there was a power plant just upstream that received barge deliveries of fuel oil two or three times a week and we were required to make sure that the passage through the bridge was clear in advance of the fuel barge's arrival and again when it came back down stream after the eight hours it usually took to pump out its cargo. The fuel barge and its tug came from New York and timed its arrivals and departures to coincide with the very top of the high tide at the railroad bridge as at any time other than right at the high water slack the strength of the current through the bridge opening made the passage too difficult. The routine was that the power plant would call the bridge tender when the tug and barge had entered the river mouth and then we would have about 45 minutes to clear everything out of the channel. Once the tug and barge had gone through I would move the equipment back into place. Of course, at the end of each day we would have to leave the opening unobstructed so I would shift the two barges around to the other side of the fender out of the channel. So, there was a lot of shifting involved in the job and it often had to be done in a hurry and regardless of how strongly the current might be running at the time.

The river was narrow and the bridge was situated at the mid-point of a broad S-curve which created a nasty cross current around the piers of the bridge. Ideally, the opening channel of a bridge should be designed so that the current runs straight through it on both the flood and ebb tides. This greatly improves the safety of the bridge for large vessels passing through, and, of course, equally protects the bridge from damage. This particular span had a bad reputation for its strong crosswise set when the current was running and evidence of that was our presence there that winter, repairing the fender after all of the passing damage that it had sustained.

But, as if the conditions of the job were not complicated enough, there was ice to contend with. Great rafts of it, as much as 18 inches thick, would come sailing down the river with every outgoing tide. It would careen into the work barges with enough impact to threaten the strength of the lines that secured the barges in place along the fender. It would strike the barges with tremendous force and then the current would sweep the ice bodily underneath the barge. You could hear it rumbling and scraping along the steel bottom until it passed and remerged downstream like a breaching whale. The steel barges were built to withstand much of this abuse, but my little tug was built of wood and more than 50 years old at that time. To tangle directly with one of these monsters could well be the end of it, so every day was a constant challenge, moving the equipment from one place to another on short notice and all the while dodging destruction at the hands of the ice.

And the worst of it was that at that time I was hopelessly inexperienced and really just making it up as I went along, all the time keeping up a brave front. I was alone on the boat and dependent on members of the construction crew to handle lines both on the tug and on the barges. This was tricky because none of them knew what to do and, so, each move required a lot of preparation in seeing that everything was set up properly in advance. It was nearly impossible to change the arrangement of lines once the tug and its barges were underway as there was no guarantee that whoever was my deckhand at that moment would be able to do what was needed. With every shift of the equipment it was necessary to figure out a way to configure the tug and barges so that the entire maneuver could be done with an absolute minimum of line handling.

It wasn't that there was a lack of useful men on the work crew. All of them were pretty handy guys; able to saw and hammer, measure, excavate, weld, and even electrify. At home I'm sure that they all repaired their own boilers and changed their own spark plugs – do it yourself guys; and that was the problem. Whenever they volunteered to help shift one of the barges they would also volunteer their own interpretation of how the job should be done. While I would be working toward one objective, they would be working toward another, or several others if there was more than one of the men involved. Lines would be unaccountably cast off in mid-stream or else secured so profusely that they would jam up tight as iron and be impossible to get undone once the job was finished. I think that the majority of the men liked to assist just for the novelty of it and whenever we made a shift there were always one or two who would pass up the chance to retire into the hooch to grab a smoke and instead would range around the deck of the tug and the barge looking for something sailorly to do.

Out of the whole crew there was really only one guy who seemed to have any talent for the basic work of line

199

handling and for the sake of my own self-preservation I undertook to teach him as much as I could. His name was Dave and he seemed to be a journeyman on the crew, general laborer and guy who got stuck with the shit work such as being sent down onto a half sunk work float to operate the big two handed air drill with the three foot auger bit for boring the bolt holes for a course of timber fendering. He was about my age, wore his hair in a short pony tail and was serious about proving himself. The older guys in the crew, the ones who would rather grab a smoke than play at being tugboat men were more than happy to let Dave do more than his share of the work, and because he seemed willing to play that role, I began to rely on him as my regular deck hand whenever there was shifting to be done. He was clearly smart and would quickly understand whatever I showed or explained to him and very soon we were operating together with a reasonable degree of coordination. In a little more time, Dave was becoming proficient enough to keep the other deckhand volunteers under control and to prevent the sorts of small disasters that had plagued the first couple of weeks of the job.

The winter was a cold one with lots of ice and frequent snow and the pace of the job suffered from the demands that the weather imposed upon us. Some days it had gone so cold overnight that it took all day to get the engines of the crane and the air compressor running. Mooring lines would be frozen to the deck or else so stiff that they could not be worked. But overall the things assumed a steady pace over each five-day work week and sometimes for me and the tug Saturdays as well, if there was maintenance that needed to be done on the equipment, in which case my services would be needed to run the maintenance crews to and from the work site. It was a good routine with the tug making money six days of the week. The work site and the old sand and gravel dock were far removed from everything, the nearest neighbor being the hulking power plant that hummed and whistled 24 hours a day; so, to be within walking distance of civilization, I would at the end of each day run about a mile downriver to tie up at the Stratford town dock, a stark nubbin of a wharf which was located about a quarter mile from a little business strip which included a deli and a pizza parlor. I would tramp back and forth between the river and the town whenever I needed supplies, pizza, or plain warmth. Had there been a saloon I would surely have spent my time there, nursing long necks and blackberry brandy, but there wasn't any such establishment nearby so I relied instead on the cheerful checkery world of pizza with its sporadic acrobatics and brick oven ambiance.

I visited the pizza joint probably more often than was decent; a brown clad pilgrim shambling into town against the setting winter sun. It was not so much the food that drew me down the road as it was the comfort of passing through the shop's jangling door into the warm aromatic space. I would order a couple of slices or maybe a meatball sub and sit me down in a window corner after taking off my coat and wool cap for the first time since dawn. I had a nodding acquaintance with the folks who ran the place, and a speaking relationship with the girl who waited on tables. I sort of haunted the place with a faint smell of diesel oil while their regular suburban clientele swept in and out mostly with take-away. I would nurse my time there for as long as possible before heading back down to the boat.

The waitress was a little simple minded, in my estimation. At first we chatted about crystals and auras, and when she learned that I was living on my boat down at the town dock she told me a story over several evenings about a sailor, a Frenchman, who had sailed alone around the world and had then spent a year tied up right where I was. The guy had obviously made a big impression on her but I couldn't tell exactly what it was. She spoke of it as a childhood memory, but being kind of childlike all the time it was hard to tell exactly where the memory lay. She and I got to be friends. I used to look forward to seeing her. I imagined that some evening she would come down to the boat and just knock on the door, but she never did.

The rest of my evenings were passed in my cabin or in the pilothouse, reading, writing by the light of the kerosene lamp until it was time to bank the stove and turn in. Then, lying in the dark, I could hear the river tide hissing past the boat's hull; from the broad marsh on the far shore I could hear the gabbling of black ducks. Sometimes it was deathly still and sometimes the wind boomed shore to shore. Located out of the main stream of the current, the dock was less exposed to the battering of the river ice, but almost always there were small bits of it quietly grinding at the hull.

I would wake each morning at first light, shake down and replenish the stove, and look out across the river to the marsh and the eastern sky to discover the day's weather. While coffee was heating up on the stove I would go out to clear any snow or ice that had formed overnight, then down into the engine room to start up. Before the sun was over the horizon I would be underway, bound upriver to the job site, arriving at the old sand yard to meet the crew, waiting in their beat up cars with plumes of exhaust fog wreathing about. I would idle into the bulkhead, jump down from the pilothouse to put out a line, then go back inside until the crew was ready to come down.

An unusual thing about this job was that, while around New York Harbor everybody would have been members of the Dockbuilders Local and all of them highly experienced in handling the marine aspects of the work, this crew from the supervisor on down to the laborers were just rock and dirt guys, accustomed to highway jobs. They knew little about working around the water and nothing prepared them for the conditions that they met on that bitter stream that winter. Up to that time, my experience tending marine construction jobs had been confined to New York where the deck bosses had years and years of experience, knew exactly what they were doing and emanated an aura of undisputed authority. On those jobs I was accustomed to being told what to do in a few quietly uttered syllables and it would then be my task to carry out those orders well enough so as not to earn the boss's tight jawed glare of disapproval. The majority of these leaders had learned a soft spoken, firmly polite manner quite at odds with the popular image of one of these waterfront centurions; orders were recast as questions, and handshakes were gentle as if candling eggs.

But this job on the Housatonic had benefit of none of that authority and experience. As far as marine practice went, it soon appeared that I was the most experienced person at hand. In fact, it became apparent that, in hiring me and my little boat from New York, I had been expected to bring with me the full text of the dock builder's bible. In fact, my expertise amounted to not much more than the biblical equivalent of a Jehovah's Witness pamphlet slipped under a breezeway door. In short, we were winging it and it was something of a miracle that the whole operation wasn't swept away with an outgoing tide.

The foreman eventually came to trust me to figure out how to make realities out of his vague expectations as to how his equipment should be arranged on the job site. Most of the effort revolved around insuring that as much of the action, equipment, and materials as possible was within the compass of the crane. Added to this was the necessity that as much of the floating equipment as possible should be protected from the battering of the ice sheets that careened up and down with the tide. Most important was to protect the low timber work float on which one of the crew had to stand, sometimes ankle deep in the icy tide, to set the

205

bolts and spikes in the lower ends of the fendering timbers. When the current was running strong and the ice was heavy it was necessary to keep a man on the deck of the barge tending a line attached to the waist of the man on the float. With the approach of a dangerous cake of ice, it was the responsibility of the man at the safe end of the rope to call the guy on the float back up onto the barge and to help, if necessary by, hauling him up by the rope. We never lost a man off the float, but twice, just as the man had scrambled up onto the barge, the float was carried away. It was usually Dave who was down on the float and so it was usually he who would jump onto the tug to go off in pursuit of the lost float, to extract it from the ice, and tow it back so that he could climb back down onto it and get back to work. At one point I remember, he asked me about a book I had been reading, tossed down on the settee in the pilothouse. It was a copy of *Far Tortuga* which I gave to him after I had finished and he said later he thought was great. He asked me what else I read and I told him he should try *White Dawn*, though I was just then getting into Faust.

Several of the crew were plainly scared of the water. They were reluctant to even walk near the edge of the barges. One of them, a Portuguese, would cross himself every morning before taking the step from dry land to the deck of the tug. Then again, when he stepped back ashore at the end of each work day he would cross himself again and mumble something to the river. The other guys would kid him about it, but it was obvious that he was serious and that his was only the most overt demonstration of concern over the risk that all of us undertook each day. The swift current, the ice and the frigid water would have made short work of any one of us who fell in.

By mid-March the job was winding down. All that was left was the trimming up of the timber structure, building of a light timber catwalk along the top of the fender wall, and reinstalling the wiring and lights that pricked out the dimensions of the bridge opening at night. The material scow was now empty; all of its cargo having gone into the new fabric of the bridge. Over one weekend I towed it back to New York then ran back out to be on the job Monday morning. Two weeks later, everything was done and I returned the crane barge to New York as well. It was a pleasure to get back to the Harbor and an even greater pleasure to be able to eat something other than pizza. I moved on to hauling scrap iron out of Newtown Creek maybe two days a week and working as deckhand on other boats when I could scare up no work of my own.

That winter on the bridge at Stratford had been a kind of turning point for me. A couple of years later I had built up enough business to be able to trade up to a bigger, more capable steel boat; perfect for the kind of towing that I did. It had been built for the navy in 1941, solid as a rock. A new engine had been installed in 1968, a 588 horsepower Cat that I grew to love. Unlike the nice little wooden boat that I had for the first years, this boat had no quarters that you could comfortably live in full-time and so after that I lived ashore, got married, had a child, ran my own business, and was happy.

***

Beyond Stratford Point the Sound widens out and becomes a lonely place. Though still protected by land on all sides the distances are great enough to give the feeling of open water with room enough for the weather to generate some real malice. And over the next two hours the wind rose. Blowing directly across the Sound from the Long Island shore, the wind created a steadily increasing chop; a foot, two feet, finally, four to six, cut short and steep by the meddling of the current. This was not a storm, nor a gale; just a breezy night with a sloppy sea, hazy inattentive stars overhead and, well after midnight, a hollow cheeked moon. It was just one of those sour nights and the tug, and the tow, Beth and I all dealt the penance of a long course rolling in the trough of the sea. For the first while I clung to my stool at the helm, but soon the effort of keeping it and myself upright became more than it was worth, and I lay the seat down flat wedged in the corner and took up a standing position propped in between the engine control and the steering stand. I had already dogged tight the door on the windward side of the pilothouse and the spray and slop pounded against it as we rolled and rolled our way along.

Outside New Haven harbor a freighter lay at anchor with all of its deck lights on. Alongside the ship lay a fuel barge attended by a Red Star tug, these, too, ablaze with light. The sizzling metallic light created a tiny hot world out in the windswept dark. Within that bright island of light the side of the ship, the glistening tug and barge, the whitecaps, and a smattering of dipping and wheeling gulls created their own small crazy world. Much larger than us and weather-cocked straight into the eye of the wind the ship, tug, and barge were riding to chop without any difficulty though the slap of the waves at their bows created the illusion that they were forging ahead rather than moored. The man on watch in the Red Star boat gave me a call on the radio to find out what boat and where I was bound. I identified my boat and told him we were headed down to Saybrook with a crane and a scow.

"Yeah," he replied, "I can just make out the lights there on the tow. Not a great night to be bringing a small tow down here. Bet you're hoping this breeze lays down a bit before you get out around Long Sand Shoal."

"Either lays down or shifts around to somewhere else. This laying right in the trough is going to get tiresome."

"I hear you, Cap. You know there's nobody on our mooring in behind the breakwater if you want to hang on there for a while 'til this settles out."

"Thanks a lot, Cap. I really appreciate that, but we've got promises to keep and I guess we'll keep going. Got a pretty good little boat here and I think she's good for it, though she surely does love to roll."

"I hear you, Cap. They're no good unless they roll some. You just keep on and be safe."

"Thank you for that and you have a good night, too."

The thought of ducking in behind the New Haven breakwater and picking up the mooring there was a real temptation. At that moment, with the first queasy hints of seasickness stirring in the muscles of my neck and jaw, and the prospect of hours more flogging our way through the dark, the idea of rocking peacefully in sheltered water was painfully attractive. But it made no sense. By the time we had run in behind the breakwater and there behind its shelter, gathered up our two barges, and then gotten secured at the mooring, it would nearly be daylight and there we would be, still with many miles of rough water confronting us, a contractor standing around in Saybrook wondering what had become of us, and the job blown all to Hell moneywise. There really wasn't a choice; just wishful thinking.

***

"Geez, whatcha' doin'?" Beth asked as she climbed up into the pilothouse hanging tight to the handrail.

"Wind's got up, I guess," I replied. "Get any sleep?"

"Oh, I slept pretty well for a while until you started rocking the boat. Then I started thinking about coffee. You want some?"

"No thanks, but I could use a Coke and a couple slices of bread."

"Comin' up," she said as she climbed back down.

Frequently, I peered behind to check on our tow. The red and green sidelights of both barges were plainly visible tracking along well downwind of the tug's wake. Wide and boxy, the two vessels corkscrewed, tossed, and heaved, but appeared to be riding well enough. At half hour intervals I would put the tug's searchlight on them and examine them with the binoculars and as best as I could tell, everything on their decks as staying put. The beam of the light formed a translucent cone that lounged astern over the tug's wake. Across its scope flew wraiths of windswept spray and the tug's exhaust. The barges gyrated crazily sometimes in unison, and then in wicked counterpoise. The cargoes lashed on deck seemed to be secure as best I could tell, and though the motion of the two vessels was considerable, there was no sign that the lines between them were overloading at any stage of their dance. Still, with the rhythm of the waves subject to the constant interplay of wind and current there was no way to tell when the fretful harmony of the tow might lapse into discord. But, for the time being at least, everything seemed to be in balance.

But on the gauge panel, dimly lit above the engine controls, one of the fuel filters was beginning to show signs of trouble. This was pretty much to be expected whenever the tug began to roll heavily, as the motion would inevitably stir up sediment gathered in the bottoms of the fuel tank and this material would lodge in the first of three filters, which in sequence ensured that only clean fuel would ever reach the engine itself. This first filter was set up with two filter canisters, either one of which could be shut off for cleaning while the other continued providing fuel to the system. When the vacuum gauge on the control panel began to show that the filter in use was beginning to clog, it was time to go down into the engine room and switch over to the other canister, then to remove the clogged element and replace it with a new one. Once the new filter was in place a little extra fuel had to be poured into the canister to displace any air and then the canister was closed up and put back in line.

I asked Beth to watch the helm while I went down to attend to the filter. The engine room was bright, hot, and loud. The space tipped and reeled crazily while the engine roared on steadily. The wrenches, hanging in order on their board over the work bench and vise, clanged and rattled to the motion. I selected the two that I would need to deal

213

with the filter and grabbed a shallow pan out of the tool cabinet to set under the filter housing to catch any spilled fuel. From a shelf in the corner I took a new filter element, pure white and crisply pleated, and then filled a small stainless steel ewer with clean fuel, and finally an empty bucket into which I would discard the clogged element. With all of these items carefully laid out I kneeled on the steel floor plates alongside the engine and set to work. I had performed this very ritual hundreds of times over the years, yet still cautioned myself to concentrate on every detail because one mistake – a valve turned the wrong way or a small part fumbled into the bilge – could spell disaster with the engine abruptly stalled or an uncontrolled fuel leak. And even discounting the small chance of a major disaster there was the annoyance of spilled fuel which seemed to always happen to some extent. This time the job went smoothly and in no time the canister was sealed back up and ready to go back on line. But the time spent in the cramped space with the heavy vapor of hot diesel fuel had taken its toll on my stomach and I ended up vomiting twice into the bilge before I finished cleaning up and putting my tools away.

"Welcome back," said Beth as I arrived in the pilothouse.

"That was no fun," I said, gulping down the cool fresh air.

"You want another Coke or anything?" she asked.

"No thanks, I'm good for now," I said, distrustful of putting anything more in my stomach for the time being. "But you can steer for a little if you like."

And so, we thrashed our way through the night; the little tug like a suit of armor against the weather buttoned up tight to protect the frail resolve within. We went about our tasks without complaint, thrown and sickened in the dim glow of the instruments and gauges, radar, GPS, chart light. The Goose Rocks and Faulkner's Island slipped past to the left and then the lighted buoy at the westward end of Long Sand Shoal to the right, and then the horizon to the east began to show as daylight gradually returned. The green flashing lighthouse at the river mouth was showing and the end was in sight.

But as we labored between the Connecticut shore and the length of Long Sand Shoal the chop changed shape under the influence of the shallow water and the strong current; and just a couple of miles short of the river mouth the two barges began to strain against one another. From the tug I could see that the second scow was veering sharply port and starboard in a cadence ever more opposite

215

to the first. At the end of each lurch the lines between the two would come up short and hard, and the scows would lurch. Immediately, I cut the tug's throttle back in an attempt to break the deadly rhythm, but nevertheless, they clashed one last time. There was a puff of steam and tatters as the line securing the downwind corners of the two scows parted with explosive recoil. The back scow swung around, still attached to the other by its windward corner but now bucking in the chop in an even more chaotic dance.

"Jeez, I fucked that up," I cursed, still peering aft with the binoculars trying to judge what steps I might take to ease the strain on what remained. Paradoxically, it appeared that a lower throttle setting was exactly the wrong medicine as it allowed the rebellious scow to range farther left and right, so I judged that a bit more engine power would keep it more in line. I nudged the throttle back up a little and, indeed the tow settled down somewhat.

"One line down, two to go," I said to Beth.

"Now I know why we went to the trouble of putting all that out yesterday."

"Hope it doesn't get down to that last one, but I'm glad it's there."

An hour later we were close enough to the river mouth that it was time to shorten up the tow wire in preparation for passing in between the twin jetties that protected the channel across the river bar. I brought the tow around to head directly into the wind while Beth went back onto the pitching stern deck to operate the towing winch. She methodically wound in the wire until the lead scow was perhaps a boat length astern of the tug, as close as we dared bring it given the sea conditions and the amount of power that I would have to use to get the tow to fall in line behind us as we threaded in between the jetties at the river mouth. With the winch shut off, Beth returned to the pilothouse, and I swung the tow around at half throttle, steering for a point about a quarter mile outside the jetties. Out here the flood current was just beginning to run against us, though I expected that the river itself, especially at this season of heavy snow melt far up in New England, would still be flowing out. I hoped to meet this outward flow just before we got between the jetties, for if there was still a strong cross current at the jetties, the stern of the second scow, trailing maybe 300 hundred feet behind the tug, could be carried down onto the west jetty. As we approached our turning point outside, we entered a plume of brownish silt-laden water, distinct from the grey-green of the Sound, a sure sign that there was indeed an outflow from the river. The outflow had an almost magical effect of calming the chop that had bedeviled us all night, and we sailed up into the protection of the river just as the sun lifted up across the horizon. The scows followed us, all docile now, though swimming all cockeyed and trailing shreds of the parted line.

We passed up into the river to a stretch just above Saybrook where the channel widened out and there we set about gathering up the tow, which took about an hour of maneuvering in the wind and current. Beth worked out on the tow while I assisted her with the tug by nudging the scows around until they were secured snugly end to end and the tug alongside. I swung the tow around and started up toward the highway bridge a mile or so upstream where we would be delivering the scows.

"Everything still in place on the scows?" I asked Beth.

"Yes, everything's right where they put it, except that one line and that's all over the place. Glad I wasn't there when it parted."

"We're lucky that's all that happened. Scow could be hanging on the end of the west jetty right now."

"Sometimes you get lucky," said Beth cheerfully.

"Yup…. I guess so."

***

We called on the radio to the Amtrak bridge between us and our destination and the bridge operator got right back to us.

"Good morning, Cap. I been watching you getting your tow straightened out down there. I'm ready to open up so you just keep coming."

We passed through and in ten minutes more were laying out in the stream right off the job site. It was maybe ten minutes to 8:00. As luck would have it, we were right on time, even a few minutes ahead. Clustered beneath the lofty highway bridge was a collection of floating equipment; several barges including a tall crane. Our two scows needed to be landed someplace among this jumble and we lay off in the stream awaiting instructions with the tug just holding the tow in place against the current. Pretty soon, three workers appeared, picking their way through the jumble of equipment on shore until they reached the upstream corner of the outermost of their flotilla. One of the men began waving his arms back and forth to indicate that he wanted our tow landed along the upstream side which was the simplest of an almost infinite number of increasingly complicated possibilities. Beth went out onto the front of the tow to give me hand signals as we edged up to the landing and then to hand the lines across as we slid into position. The construction guy directed us in from his position on the work site. By the way he directed the operation you could see that he had some experience with marine work which is always a welcome sight.

As soon as we were tied up, the guy stepped across onto the front of our tow and made his way back toward the tug. Though he didn't make a show of it, I could see that he was inspecting the gear lashed down on deck to check for any loss or damage. He paused for a minute to look at the wreckage of the line we had parted just before dawn, then he stepped aboard the tug and I opened the door to let him into the pilothouse.

He wasn't an especially big guy but as with many foremen he occupied a lot of space. He had longish blond hair, streaked with the grey of age and time outdoors. His face was deeply weathered and his gaze direct.

"Good morning," he said. "I didn't know if you were going to get here with this wind and all."

"It wasn't great, but we were able to keep going."

"I drove down to the point early this morning to see if I could see you coming in. Looks like you had a little trouble there."

"Oh yeah, coming out the East River last night it looked like it was maybe going to blow so we put out a bunch of extra line. That one you saw broken up there was one of mine."

"Whatever gets it here safe…. Take a line off the deck here to replace it if you want. My guys fuck up so many lines around here one more will never be missed."

"Thanks, I'm good."

"You going to lay here a while for the weather to settle down or you headed back?"

"I'll be shutting down for a couple of minutes to go over the engine, then we'll be gone. We'll work our way across to the Long Island side and it'll be fine."

"Well, you're welcome to lay here as long as you like."

"Thanks," I said.

"Hey," the foreman asked just as he as turning to go, "There used to be a guy, years ago, worked out of New York on bridge jobs out here. Lived on his boat by himself; used to read and write on his time off. You know who I'm talking about?"

"That was me," I replied and he scrutinized my face.

"Nooo… You're not him," he said.

"You Dave?" I asked.

"Yeah, I'm Dave, but I don't think you're him," and he went back out to work.

***

Outbound from the river running light we skirted around the east end of Long Sand Shoal. It was rough there, but steaming straight into the wind we punched through it and were soon under the lee of the Long Island shore where it smoothed out. From there we bore west back to New York. Beth steered for a couple of hours while I caught a nap, then we ate sandwiches, and around 5:00 that afternoon we were back in the Harbor.

Jamaica Bay Subway Bridge

Enchantment can be a problem in Jamaica Bay. Compared to most everywhere else in New York Harbor it is completely open to the sky and the wind hisses over it with abandon. It is a disorienting place with a puzzle of small channels through a myriad of marsh. The brushy shores make a maze of secret paths. Slowly drowning colonies of stilt shanties teeter in the coves, eel trappers prowl the flats, and fishermen equipped with white plastic pails, boom boxes, and springy 12 foot poles might appear anywhere at any time out of the brush to practice optimism for a while on the windy shore.

But the principal feature of the Bay is the overlying sky and everything in it. JFK occupies the east shore of the bay and the air traffic is constant, capped twice a day by the rolling thunderclap of the Concorde's departure; lancing out low and flat over the marsh, then throttling up out over the ocean to an unbelievable pitch and attack to scale away across the Atlantic.

But even without the jets, the skies are full of souls. Birds swirl everywhere, and in late winter vast flocks of migrant waterfowl gather in the open water. Canada geese, of course, in their solemn formations, but also tribes of smaller Brant and above all the cackley clouds of snow geese looking for all the world like wind tossed confetti or fine blown ash.

I worked for a year, off and on, at a project rebuilding the Jamaica Bay subway bridges, two antique iron swings, way out on the far end of the A train; about as far from song as you can get. One of the bridges spanned the North Channel hard by the bitter little enclave of Howard Beach and the other all the way across at the Breezy Point side spanning Beach Channel. Between the two bridges stretches a low uninhabited island fringed all around with salt marsh and tidal flat.

Navigating through the marsh can be tricky. The terrain is a low and uniform tapestry of *Spartina*. The waters are constantly redefined by the rise and fall of tides and the perpetual shifting of the passages. It is easy to become disoriented and not unusual to get aground. Sand bars form and creep while peat banks collapse from week to week. The creeks twist and curve so that there are moments when your goal, in plain sight across the marsh, lies first off to the right, then left, then right behind.

Once, given the assignment of taking a barge into the farthest extremity of Jamaica Bay, I got lost. Never having gone there before I threaded through the maze of passages with chart at hand, struggling to tease reassurance from the twists and turns on the paper on my lap. As I went ever deeper into the maze I struggled to square my increasing bafflement with the graphic certainty of the chart, willing each twist and minutely rendered turn on the map to conform to what I actually saw before me and my ever-darker misgiving. I ended up in an unmarked, unnamed, and unnavigable side channel. (Shit Creek, perhaps?) Admitting that I was completely lost, I stopped before running into the marsh and spent the next hour laboriously backing the tug and tow out of my dead end and re-gathering my humbled wits.

Around this time it was all over the news that there was a tug captain bound for the first time for the port of Providence, Rhode Island. He was pushing a fully loaded oil barge up Narragansett Bay, in broad daylight, and somehow mistook the broad passage leading instead up Mount Hope Bay into the Port of Fall River. As he proceeded ever farther off course he was able to convince himself that he was still on course until he arrived in the wrong port and began calling on the radio to locate the terminal where he was scheduled to unload. The marine community was astonished and horrified. The Coast Guard was inflamed; and the poor captain was an unemployable laughing-stock. Because of my own experience in Jamaica Bay I personally could not mock him, a brother victim of self-enchantment.

My role in the repair of the subway bridges was to bring floating equipment back and forth between the job site and New York harbor, and then to shift that same equipment. Sometimes I was called down to the job site just to move the floating equipment from place to place around each job site or at other times to move equipment from one bridge site to the other. These assignments might turn out to be just an hour or so of work, added of course to the time spent running all the way down there and back; then sometimes I might be down there for two or three days if there was a lot of shifting to be done. On those occasions, there was quite a bit of down time and then of course the overnight. That kind of slow moving job makes it possible to really get to know a patch of the harbor, better than just passing through it now and then.

In winter, as I've said there were the birds, dispersing into the marshes to feed at nightfall, then regathering in the safety of open water at dawn. In summer it was more the fish than fowl; bluefish, summer flounder, scup, striped bass. I kept a fish pole on board and sometimes caught our dinner there in the evenings after everything quieted down and the flood current swirled through the ancient footings of the bridge. Being down there for a day or two was sort of like a small paid vacation for Beth and me.

So, on the day in question, the work day started with a shift of one of the scows into the opening of the bridge on the Breezy Point side. The week before we had set a middling sized hydraulic crane with a telescoping boom onto that scow specifically to extract a heavy D.C. electric motor from its mounting deep underneath the turntable of the bridge span. The motor was situated beneath the subway tracks in what amounted to a crawl space deep in the internals of the bridge structure. The plan was to place the barge under the bridge at exactly the right stage of the tide so that the boom of the crane could be extended deep into this confined space, hook up the motor and lift it just enough to free it from its mountings, then retract the boom to pluck the motor out from under the span and onto the barge so that it could be transported on the barge back to Brooklyn, and put ashore to be rebuilt.

One of the ironworkers crawled into the space to give hand signals as, lovingly, the crane operator inserted the boom of the crane until the tip of it was right over the motor and the hook-up ready to be made. The iron worker was just moving to take hold of the hoisting block and hook it to the lifting eye on top of the motor when some part of the crane's boom came in contact with the subway voltage. A tremendous clap of lightning, smoke and molten metal thundered out of the crawl space. The spray of liquid steel and copper spattered across the deck of the barge as if blasted directly out of Hell and we all stood astonished and dumb as the hot gray pall of smoke continued to roll out from under the bridge. One man grabbed a fire extinguisher and ran toward the disaster while another, as if acting in a silent movie fervently grappled him back from fear of instant electrocution.

And then he reappeared! He came rolling out of the smoke, crabwise scrambling, hard hat gone, Carhartt jacket smoldering. He tumbled from the stone abutment to the deck of the barge, regained his feet and fled to the farthest most corner, away from everyone and everything, sat himself down on top of the corner bit there and lit a cigarette, breathing hard and staring wildly off across the marsh toward the sky and all the gabbling birds.

One of us who were witness said, "I saw fucking smoke coming out of his mouth."

Another, "Should'a been dead, all I'm tellin' ya."

The A line was out of service for the rest of the day. A host of suited officials came and went. Eventually, we took advantage of the power being out to have another go at getting the motor out of there and were successful. The freshly enchanted man remained the rest of the day on the corner of the scow. He would talk to no one, waving away anyone who approached. He smoked one cigarette after another, lighting each from the butt of the one before until he ran out and then the other iron workers gave him several packs of their own.

A Tail

Down at the foot of Pearl Street, right down at the Battery, there's a tall glass building the face of which is curved to suggest the arc of the sun as it rises daily from the East River, stares straight into the eyes of the Statue at noon, and finally lays down to rest in Bayonne. The building's face is clad in silvery glass which has the knack of assuming every day the tenor of the harbor and the tone of the sky. When it was first constructed in the early 80's, as I passed it every day with one tow or another, I dismissed the building as the sort of thing that might play well in the sticks but was far too introspective for the haughty aesthetics of New York. But with time I grew to love the way that the building's simple curvature braved nothing more nor less than the essence of each day.

But there is something more to that building than its serene presence. Its footprint occupies several ancient lots; one of which happens to be the spot where Herman Melville lived as a child. Number 6 Pearl Street was his home and the environs of Lower Manhattan were his earliest dream-scape. A very different city then, small and lamp-lit, less ambiguous in its brutalities, its truths and its humiliations.

When the gentle mirrored building at the foot of Pearl Street began construction there was the inevitable demolition of the older generation of structures in its place; and these as best as I can remember were modest brick office buildings dating from around 1900; each 12 to 20 stories tall and to all but the souls who had scribbled their lives away inside them, anonymous. The Melville home had disappeared in an earlier round of development, but in the peculiar way of the New York cycle of building and demolition, the original home had left its north wall embossed on the side of the middle generation building that had at some time in the late 19th century shouldered up beside it. There, stuck to the exterior wall of the office building was the interior wall of the 18th century house that had been, cheek by jowl, its neighbor. The plaster walls of the ancestral building were still intact, painted and papered each room and floor by floor a different color. In the few days between the moment when the ongoing demolition revealed this relic and the day when it too was finally demolished, I visited the site, peeping through the plywood construction barricade. I was curious to see if there was anything to be learned? In some ghost closet a white chalk scribble of a whale? Or secreted in a chink, a cannibal tar baby? Within a day or two the memory wall was dust and the evidence, if ever there was, gone.

***

I was at a party in a loft on Warren Street when a friend introduced a couple to me. Jonathan Baranik and his wife Suzanne. My friend who had brought them over introduced them, explaining that they had a favor to ask and that they had already told her it was absolutely OK if I said no. It was a lot to ask, they knew. But did I ever hire out to take people out into the harbor? You see, Jonathan stammered, might it be possible to hire me and my boat to scatter some ashes out by the Statue of Liberty? - a surprisingly common request.

"Who's ashes?" I asked.

"Suze's Mom," Jonathan replied glancing regardfully at his wife.

"How many?" I asked.

Jonathan hesitated, "Just one," he eventually replied.

I stared at him and he stared at me and then he continued, "No I meant just her Mom...her ashes I mean.

There would be four of us, Suzanne, her Mom's two sisters and me."

"That sounds easy enough. When are you thinking to do it? Can you do it tomorrow? Show up around 1130 and we're on."

"That would be wonderful," Suzanne said, "I'm going to bring some sandwiches and something to drink and, oh yes, I have to ask what it will cost."

By rights I could have demanded the coins with which they had at the last weighted down her eyelids but I demurred.

"It doesn't really cost me anything," I told her. "Just bring along an extra sandwich and we'll call it even."

Next morning, right on time, they appeared at the foot of the pier; four cautious figures moving from the disarray of city traffic into the bright sun of the open pier. Jonathan led the way while the others clung to one another two steps behind. Suzanne, tall and confident, held the center with a tiny ancient woman on each arm. Jonathan, out ahead of them carried in one hand a small picnic cooler and in the other hand a sturdy public radio tote bag. He had warned me that the two sisters were very old and as a precaution I had scrounged two pressed wood chairs from the bar up the street and had lashed each of these to the towing bitts at the stern. Jonathan, Suzanne, and I carefully transferred the two old folks from the dock to the boat and into their chairs. They were soft, warm, surprisingly heavy, yet tiny. Once seated their feet barely touched the deck.

Suzanne introduced us. "These are Mom's two sisters, Rachel and Miriam. Rachel, this is the tugboat captain we told you about."

Rachel stared up at me with red rheumy eyes, "So he takes us to the cemetery?"

"No, Aunt Ray, don't you remember? Mom said she didn't want the cemetery."

"She never told me that," Rachel countered and Suzanne ignored.

"And Aunt Miriam," Suzanne continued bravely," this is the man who's going to take us out into the harbor." "This is all outside," Miriam observed. "Where's the inside?"

"Your mother didn't know anything from any tugboat," Rachel growled, scanning left and right from her little throne.

"But Aunt Ray, didn't Mom always talk about how granddad came here on the ship and about seeing the Statue for the first time?"

"Acch! He said it was like cattle," Rachel spat back.

"Well Dad always said it was the best day of their life," Suzanne pleaded.

"He was an idiot, and your mother knew it," Miriam declared as Jonathan glanced at me and rolled his eyes.

"OK"' I said. "Now, we're just going to go out into the harbor for a little bit to find a good place and if you all just hang out here until we get there."

We pulled away from the pier, headed down the East River, around the Battery and over toward the Jersey side to get up close to the Statue. Looking back to the stern I could see Suzanne hovering over the ladies, buttoning and unbuttoning their jackets, extracting a broad brimmed gardener's hat from a bag and planting it on Miriam's head only to have her reach up with a clawed hand and distractedly brush it away. Meanwhile, Jonathan stood by the rail hopefully pointing out things on shore, trying manfully to distract the ladies from their gloom. Before long he gave up and made his way forward to plan out our next move.

"Thank you for doing this," he began. "It means a lot to Suzanne."

"Oh, it's a pleasure. I just wish that Miriam and Rachel were a little more comfortable."

"Oh, they're OK. They just didn't know about any of this until we called them last night and I guess they had something else in mind. Suzanne says that this is what her Mom wanted. She could see a little sliver of the water from her apartment and she always used to watch it for boats going by, so this is good."

"Well, we're just about there. I can stop the boat anywhere in here if you like and you can do your thing back on the stern. Just tell me where you want to be.

"I think maybe up here kind of mid-way between the Statue of Liberty and Ellis Island if that's OK?"

"Sure. I'll swing the boat around so from back there you've got a good view. Take all the time like and I'll be up here if you need anything."

It was just noon and the day was hot and hazy. There was no breeze at all, but as the afternoon came on there would surely be a sea breeze sweeping up through the Narrows. The tide was nearly high and the last of the flood current drew us northward toward Ellis Island maybe just as the once young woman we were about to lay to rest had been drawn as a young woman so many years ago. I looked back toward the stern to see my guests clustered together, holding hands, the old ladies still seated. They appeared to be muttering among themselves and after a few minutes of this they all made a clumsy effort to embrace. Suzanne and Jonathan made a good job of it, but when the two of them bent to hug the aunts they were only able to grapple with their crowns and muffle their ears with their forearms. But then, once the children had withdrawn the two ancients guardedly reached out to touch then briefly twine their gnarly fingers

And then they got down to the heart of the thing. Suzanne knelt on the deck and from the tote bag that Jonathan had brought she lifted the receptacle. It was fashioned of some grade of plasticized cardboard which looked for all the world like polished steel. A radiant, inscrutable cube. Unless he was going to break into the thing using his teeth, he was going to need a knife and I was just reaching into my pocket for my jack knife when he turned dramatically toward the Statue, knelt against the tugboat's rail and solemnly dropped the mystery over the side – intact.

"Oh Damn," said I as a stray current drew the box back under the stern of the boat where it hid. The little family repeated the hugging and hand holding thing for a little while and then Jonathan came back up to the pilothouse. He told me that they were all done and that we could head back. I tried to get them to come up forward for the ride back so that I could safely get away, but Jonathan thought better of the old ones trying to walk the deck, so I began to back the tug away from the spot hoping that maybe the box would get sucked through the tug's propeller or, failing that, we might at least get far enough away from it so that none of my guests would see what had not become of the departed. As soon as Jonathan moved to rejoin his family, I put the boat in reverse and, answering my worst fear, the gaily buoyant cube emerged from close alongside to dervish off my bow. I continued to back away for what I hoped was a safe distance then levered the boat into forward gear to swing around for home. I was just beginning to think that I had succeeded when Suzanne turned around to take one last fond look at the Statue and the object caught her eye.

"Let it go," I whispered to myself., "Please let it go."

But she didn't. Pointing urgently, she grabbed Jonathan's arm and that sudden move alarmed the aunts who then were also pointing, open mouthed, wide eyed so that I could almost hear them crying:

Thar she blows!

"We've got to get her back!" Jonathan cried, and we circled around to do just that, but everything conspired against us. The deck of the tug was just too far off the water for hands to reach it, so no matter how close I was able to maneuver the boat the precious object proved untouchable.

"Maybe it's leaking just a little and it will sink," Suzanne hoped after an hour of futile pursuit, but the trim of the little box showed no sign of demise.

Jonathan volunteered to jump over the side to grapple with it, but Suzanne forbade it.

Miriam and Rachel slumped dejectedly with their faces in their hands.

The box bobbed northward at a jaunty angle, looking like a stylish hat. Like a naughty puppy it toyed with all of our efforts to recover it, and so, we pursued it upstream until the tide turned and our little burlesque merged with the ebb and headed back toward the salt. The sea breeze had arrived and as always happens in the harbor when wind and current are at odds, the water surface separated into bands of greater and lesser motion and in this way create windrows and seams, and into these seams the various species of flotsam and jetsam sorted themselves according to buoyancy and windage. Oil and sullen detritus forms into one distinct band while the lighter stuff will tack and jibe around until it collects in its own discrete regiment. This afternoon, in the conditions that prevailed at the time, our flirtatious box found community among styrofoam coffee cups which it gathered around from far and wide until it was swanning down the wind in consort with a dozen of these little cherubs.

About this time one of the big Moran tugs passed with a loaded cement barge from far up the Hudson. In a dry, tired voice he called me on the radio, "What'cha got there, Cap?"

"I'm trying to sink something that doesn't want to sink."

'My experience is usually the other way around," he replied. "I was thinking maybe your cat's gone overboard but now I see what you're doing. We done that onboard here for some of the old timers now and then. It's a bitch; dust all over the place. You're picking the stuff out of your teeth for a week afterward, but you just let the box go float like you done you got to put a couple of holes in it or else it's NEVER gonna sink. I know that! Only thing to do now you got to take your pike pole and you got to stab it."

"I think you're right."

"I know I'm right. It's your pike pole or nothing," and he continued on down the river.

A pike pole is a dock builder's tool consisting of a 12 or 14 foot spruce pole with an iron fitting on the end comprised of a square tapered point which in forging has been twisted to produce a coarse screw thread point and, below that, a broad sharpened hook, like an ordinary boat hook but longer and more medieval. I got mine down from the deck-house roof and bestowed it on Jonathan.

"I'll get you close and you try to poke a hole in it."

"Oh God," he said while back in the stern the ladies sat as if cast in stone. "Not funny,"

"It will be someday, trust me," I replied.

***

Jonathan stood at the very bow, one knee braced against the rail as I maneuvered the tug into range. "Wait!... Wait... A little closer.... NOW!" And Jonathan reared back and jabbed with all his force only to see the point glance off as the box skittered away unscathed. So it continued over and over again as the cremains led us a merry chase down the harbor.

But even as our blind pursuit went on, the end was approaching. The wind and current were steadily pushing the cubical imp closer and closer toward shore, and it was clear that our quarry would soon blow ashore upon a wasted rocky shore of Jersey City where the shallow depth of the water, not to mention the rocks would put it entirely and forever out of our reach.

And worse still, there on the debris strewn shore, a little pack of boys had begun to assemble. In a loosely organized foraging party they had been rummaging along the beach, breaking bottles, overturning driftwood to investigate what might lie beneath; their destructive instincts unfocused but now, like a pack of feral dogs their attention had coalesced. They moved down to the shoreline, pointing at us, heads cocked, nosing the air for mischief. One of them bent to the ground, came up with a stone and with two quick skips forward, hurled it in our direction. It fell well short but the others in the group took the lead of the first and soon there was a hail of stones ranging toward us as we approached the shore. Suzanne had come forward to stand behind Jonathan with her hand on his shoulder as he stabbed at his mother in law with the pike.

"Don't let them get her, Jon," she hissed. "Please don't let them get her."

We drifted ever closer to the shore, into water evermore shallow until I felt the bow of the tug ground softly on soft bottom. I could go no further and I would not have even if I could as there was no way I was going to sail into that proto-humans fusillade. I left the pilothouse to see

243

if there was anything more to be done, but the object had drifted ahead beyond our reach.

Rachel and Miriam had struggled out of their seats and staggered forward. They keened and moaned and Jonathan was near to tears, when Suzanne seized the pike pole from his hands, strode to the prow, reared back, and with an animal shriek, let fly.

Never since that time below the walls of Troy were throw so true. The spear arced across the widening watery gap, arrowed straight and limber. The lance reached its zenith, then hove downward, trembling with the soul of the thrower, and struck its target clean and true.

We all stood speechless. Suzanne's chest heaved in victory, Jonathan's eyes were afire with unbounded love; and Rachel said to Miriam:

"I'll never understand why she married him."

And the little savages on shore rolled on the ground in cartoonish baboonish laughter. Like the Death Star in Episode IV the faux metallic terror was sundered; penetrated through and through, and burst in every plane. Left in its place was a chalky cloud that blanched a milky phantom in the body of the sea.

"Rest in peace, Mom," Suzanne breathed and it was over. We steamed back to the dock past the Battery and the modest skyscraper at the foot of Pearl Street that reflects the heavens.

***

Now, back in the old whaling days, the captains used hand carved stamps to record in the margins of their log books to summarize the detailed events contained in the manuscript pages. To make it easier to tally up the loss or profit at the end of each voyage each kill was marked by an inked impression of a whale and alongside it a notation of the number of barrels of oil rendered from it. There were also stamps to represent the different species of whale sighted and to represented whales engaged in battle but that had ultimately escaped. These last were commonly represented by a stamp which showed the tail of a diving whale in silhouette, poised against the sky in defiant farewell. I suppose that if this account were written in the old iconography it would end with just such a tail.

High Wire

Back in the Kills, near the Isle of Dogs, there's a power line
strung over the channel. So as not to interfere with the
shipping passing under it, it is elevated 165 feet above the
high water mark – a very generous clearance. It crosses
about a half a mile south of the blind curve in the channel
at Elizabethport and the Arthur Kill Bridge. In the other
direction, there's an equally blind curve at Tremley Point.
Because it is situated more or less mid-way between these
two blind spots it has served for many years as a radio
check-in point for commercial vessels passing under it.
Any vessel arriving at a point directly under the power line
is expected by Coast Guard regulation in the Port to
broadcast its presence along with its speed and direction of
travel on VHF radio channel 13. If that vessel happens to
be a tug it is also expected to describe what it is towing and
whether the tow is being pushed, pulled, or alongside. Any
other vessel which will soon be negotiating either of those
blind curves to meet the vessel calling from under the
power line is expected to respond and to arrange a safe
passing. By custom and regulation the check-in point is
identified variously as "the high wires" or just "the wires"

and modified as appropriate such as "north-bound under the wires".

Now, one breezy morning, I was southbound in the Kills with a small scow alongside. There's a lot to see back there but not much of it nice.

There is a steady stream of jets coming in and out of Newark, screaming down their smoky tunnel in the sky bound back and forth to ditheration. And there's the refinery stacks farting out black tar. Vast chemical plants flaunting their big stainless-steel testicles, and everything set in a world of what for lack of a better term you'd have to call robot vomit…

…and us with our little tow with the tide at our backs, making good time, when I noticed that right at the middle of the span, at the lowest point of its catenary, a gull had managed to collide; and, by misfortune, its wing had shattered and folded over the wire. The bird hung entangled up there fluttering helplessly with its one good wing. Though gulls are hardy birds, it surely did not survive for long, two or three days at most, but its dry tattered remains hung there for years like the shriveled carcasses of traitors, thieves, and thinkers over ancient city gates. In some lights you can see the wire plainly, but in other weather it's not apparent just how the gull is poised up there so obviously

248

broken winged but refusing to fall. They say that gulls are the ghosts of dead seamen, but I hope for all our sakes there's someplace better angels.

*****

Acknowledgments

My career as a tugboatman seems to me now as close to accidental as an obsession can be. The thing that led me to it was a broad fascination with seamanship which I discovered in pure form in New York Harbor. Not the seamanship of clever knots and salty language but of honor, self-discipline, and generosity, there welded to the deep traditions of sail, then steam, then diesel; as grandfather, father, son. I was blessed to be admitted into these traditions by elders who through study, trial, and hilarity had much they willed to give me; for this my humble thanks.

William Paparella, Richard Forster, Bryce Kirke and Bob White, Fred Kosnac Sr., Jr., & III, Charlie Chillemi, Pam Hepburn, John Noble, Bill Hughes, and Ken Bemish are only a partial listing of those whose stories and expertise made my life possible and these stories what I hope will serve as a memorial to themselves and to that part of the intricate and beautiful world that we all inhabit.

To my wife, Adele and son, Evan I am indebted to for their advice and patience,

To Paul Feldstein, my agent and friend, for his enduring commitment to this work,

To Brian McAllister for his early and persistent encouragement,

And, lastly, to all the men and women whose stories, lives, and – finally – names are writ in water.

Made in the USA
Las Vegas, NV
04 February 2021

16954413R00144